GLOUCESTER
A Pictorial History

The *New Inn*, drawn by Cecil Aldin.

GLOUCESTER
A Pictorial History

John Juřica

Phillimore

1994

Published by
PHILLIMORE & CO. LTD.,
Shopwyke Manor Barn, Chichester, West Sussex

ISBN 0 85033 836 0

Printed and bound in Great Britain by
BIDDLES LTD.
Guildford, Surrey

To my mother Joyce

List of Illustrations

Frontispiece: The *New Inn*

Acknowledgements

In compiling this book I have drawn extensively on research for a history of Gloucester published in volume IV of the *Victoria History of Gloucestershire* in 1988. Selection of the illustrations published here has been possible only with the assistance of many people, notably the staff of Gloucester City Library and especially Graham Baker and Christine Turton of the local history section. They deserve my utmost thanks for their help and for the patience they have shown in this endeavour. I would also like to thank Roy Jamieson of the British Waterways Archive and my colleagues in the Gloucestershire Record Office, particularly the county archivist, David Smith, for obtaining the permissions to reproduce some photographs and Debbie Allen for ensuring that the illustrations were presented suitably to the publisher. Noel Osborne of Phillimore & Co. Ltd. is also to be thanked for his forbearance during the numerous delays in this venture and his assistance in its final stages. Peter Arnold, Hugh Conway-Jones, Bruce Stait and Colin Stanley have given me invaluable help and advice. Copy photography was by Richard Hookway and Robert Rudge of Impact Photography, Cheltenham.

For permission to reproduce illustrations I would like to thank Gloucestershire County Library for items in the Gloucestershire Collection in Gloucester City Library, 4, 6, 9, 13, 17, 19-20, 22, 29-32, 34, 43-4, 46-9, 52, 57, 60, 63, 65, 69, 73-4, 79-82, 87-9, 91, 96-7, 102, 105, 110-11, 116-18, 122, 126, 129, 133 (photograph by the late Gwladys Davies), 139-40, 142-3, 145-6, 149-52, 155, 157, 160-2, 164-5, 168, 170; Mrs. Jenny James for items in the Walwin Photographic Negative Collection in Gloucester City Library, 23, 108, 121; Gloucestershire Record Office, 21, 24-7, 36-9, 41-2, 58-9, 62, 64, 66-8, 76, 84, 86, 93-4, 99, 106, 109, 113, 115, 131, 138, 153-4, 163, 171; Barnwood House Trust, 107; Tibberton Court Association Ltd., 169; the incumbent and church council of St James's parish, Gloucester, 114, 156; British Waterways Archive, 8, 11, 14, 167; Royal Commission on the Historical Monuments of England, 12, 53, 55, 77, 95, 98, 124-5; and Nicholas Herbert, editor of the *Victoria History of Gloucestershire*, 1-2, 5, 7, 10, 54, 71, 90, 100, 103, 120, 123, 127, 130, 135, 144, 147.

I am also indebted for their generosity and assistance to Margery Etheridge, 137 (from the papers of her late husband Harold Etheridge); Brian Frith, 40; Ken and Michael Hill, 15; Mr. R.H. Hinder, 28; Mr. and Mrs. Paul Mayne, 16 and 159 (from the papers of Mrs. Mayne's late father Alf Thomas); John Rowden, 18, 45, 61, 70, 72, 78, 83, 85, 104, 128, 134; and Reg Woolford, 50-1, 75, 92, 112, 141. Other illustrations are from the *Cheltenham Chronicle and Gloucestershire Graphic*, 33, 35, 119, 132, 136, 148, 158, 166; R. Philip, *Life and Times of the Revd. George Whitefield* (1842), 56, 106; and *Records of Gloucester Cathedral*, ed. W. Bazeley, volume two (1883-4), 3.

Introduction

Early Gloucester

The city of Gloucester stands at an ancient crossing-point of the river Severn and until the opening of the Severn bridge near Bristol in 1966 it was on the most southerly road into South Wales. The strategic importance of the crossing led the Romans to settle at Gloucester in the first century A.D. and after a decade they abandoned their first fort, at Kingsholm, for another site a short distance to the south. The Roman town was the precursor of an Anglo-Saxon settlement, which became an important commercial centre. The choice of Gloucester in the later seventh century as the site for a minster confirmed or established the town as a regional centre, a status enhanced *c*.900 when Ethelfleda of Mercia founded a new minster there. The first Norman kings, William I and William II, usually celebrated Christmas at Gloucester, the festival being one of the occasions on which they ceremonially wore the crown, and it was from Gloucester in 1085 that William I ordered the compilation of Domesday Book. In the Middle Ages Gloucester's leading inhabitants obtained a degree of autonomy for the town or borough in a series of royal grants culminating in a charter of 1483 which conferred on the town and the surrounding countryside the status of a separate county, known as the inshire, under the control of the mayor and aldermen. The town acquired the status of a city in 1541 on the founding of the see of Gloucester with the former abbey church of St Peter as its cathedral.

During the Civil War the city was a parliamentary stronghold and the failure of royalist troops led by Charles I to capture it by siege in 1643 was a decisive setback for his cause. Royalist retribution after the Restoration of 1660 included the demolition of the town's medieval walls and the return of the surrounding countryside to the jurisdiction of Gloucestershire. The city remained a county in its own right as well as the county town of Gloucestershire. After the turbulence of the mid 17th century Gloucester became a quiet provincial city and industrial growth, which for many comparable towns began in the later 18th century, was delayed until the early 19th century.

Georgian Gloucester

In the mid-18th century Gloucester was a compact and relatively small town. In area it was smaller than before 1643 when many of the suburbs outside the walls had been deliberately burned to protect the city from the besieging royalist army. The street pattern of the Georgian city was based on four main streets laid out, in Roman fashion, on a cruciform plan and meeting at the Cross, and it included many side lanes and alleys of medieval origin. Westgate Street, the longest of the principal thoroughfares, descended to the eastern

arm of the Severn where Westgate bridge marked the western limit of the town. The bottom part of the street between Dockham ditch, crossed by the Foreign bridge, and Westgate bridge was called the Island. Dockham ditch, also known as the Old Severn, marked a third channel in which the river had once flowed past Gloucester. In the south-west part of the city overlooking the river the county gaol occupied the keep of Gloucester's medieval castle. The north-west part of the city was dominated by the cathedral close, which under the jurisdiction of the dean and chapter retained a degree of independence from the rest of Gloucester.

Gloucester's economy depended on its rôle as a regional centre providing markets for livestock and agricultural produce, supplying goods and services to a large rural area extending beyond north Gloucestershire, and supporting traditional industries such as pinmaking, woolstapling and malting. It benefited considerably from its river trade, which was conducted at the city quay some way below Westgate bridge and upstream of the county gaol. The river trade handled agricultural produce from the surrounding countryside and local manufactures and brought imports from Bristol, goods from South Wales, and coal and industrial products from the West Midlands for distribution to surrounding towns and villages. Some timber from the Baltic was unloaded at the quay but maritime trade was severely restricted by the

1 The octagonal medieval High Cross at the centre of Gloucester served as a conduit for water piped from Robins Wood Hill in the mid 15th century and displayed statues of seven monarchs and one queen consort in the early 18th century. The Cross was removed in 1751 because it obstructed traffic. In this view of 1750 the Tolsey, the meeting place of the city council, is on the left.

hazards sea-going craft faced in the estuary immediately below the city and by the control that the neighbouring port of Bristol exercised over Gloucester's trade. Bristol's commercial dominance also stifled local attempts to start new industries and contributed significantly to the failure of Gloucester's economy to expand in the 18th century. Gloucester's regional importance was enhanced by its status as a county town and cathedral city. Although social events were held for the local gentry and leading citizens Gloucester declined as a resort for the gentry and by the end of the 18th century it was overshadowed in popularity by the neighbouring and fashionable spa town of Cheltenham.

Despite economic stagnation Gloucester's townscape changed considerably in the Georgian period. The appearance of the main streets and cathedral close, dominated by gabled timber buildings in 1714, altered as houses were rebuilt or refronted in brick. The façades of several houses and some of the chief inns were embellished but most of the new fronts were plain. The prospects of the main streets were enriched by new public buildings, namely the Tolsey, the seat of city government, at the Cross in 1751 and produce markets in Southgate and Eastgate Streets in 1786. Among the more imposing buildings of the early 19th century were several new banks, the new Bluecoat school in Eastgate Street, completed in 1808, and the Shire Hall in Westgate Street, completed in 1816. Of the city's parish churches St John the Baptist in Northgate Street was rebuilt in the years 1732-4. The other churches, St Mary de Crypt in Southgate Street, St Mary de Lode west of the cathedral precinct, St Michael at the Cross, and St Nicholas in lower Westgate Street, all retained their medieval character in the late 18th century. Six other parish churches, declared redundant in 1648, had been pulled down in the mid 17th century apart from the tower of Holy Trinity church in the centre of Westgate Street. A new church for St Aldate's parish opened in 1756 in St Aldate Street, leading off Northgate Street. In the Island the hospital of St Bartholomew, an almshouse founded in the Middle Ages, was rebuilt in the years 1787-90. Elsewhere the castle keep was pulled down in 1787 to make way for a new county gaol.

In the later 18th century several buildings were demolished to ease the movement of traffic in the city and the main streets were improved. Congestion was greatest around the Cross and in 1751 the medieval cross there, buildings in the centre of Westgate Street including Holy Trinity tower, and some buildings in Northgate and Southgate Streets were pulled down. Other obstructions near the Cross, including small houses and shops along the

2 Gloucester occupied a prominent position controlling a crossing of the river Severn. Westgate bridge, one of the structures carrying the road to South Wales across the river and the meadows of Alney Island, marked the western end of the medieval town and the massive gate leading to it remained standing until 1805 or 1806. The bridge, which in the later 18th century had four irregular spans, one formed of wooden planks, was replaced by a single stone arch completed in 1816.

north side of St Michael's church, were removed later. The medieval town gates which had survived the destruction of the walls in the early 1660s were also demolished. The west gate leading to Westgate bridge survived until 1805 or 1806.

Gloucester's population grew modestly in the 18th century and most people were housed within existing buildings or in new buildings within the city. Larger new houses built from the late 17th century were usually outside the main streets. Several were in the inner part of Barton Street, beyond the east gate, and a nonconformist chapel was erected there in 1699. Further along Barton Street, where buildings had not been put to the torch in 1643, houses were strung out and formed a roadside suburb, which at the end of the 18th century extended beyond the junctions of Goose Lane (later Millbrook Street) and India Road as far as the *Chequers* inn. The area beyond India Road was known as the World's End. Outside the south gate buildings in lower Southgate Street, the Bristol road, included a chapel erected in 1730 and the county infirmary completed in 1761. North-east of the city there were a few houses on the London road and near Wotton were the medieval almshouses or hospitals of St Margaret and St Mary Magdalen. In 1792 a small Roman Catholic chapel opened behind a house at the city end of the road.

The Growth of an Industrial City

In 1791 the arrival at the city quay of a ship bringing wine from Oporto opened up a direct trade with the Iberian peninsula and revived plans for a canal to bypass the hazardous stretches of the Severn estuary below Gloucester. A scheme for a waterway leading from the river in Berkeley to a basin on the south side of the city received strong backing locally and in the West Midlands, where much trade depended on the Severn navigation, and in 1794 construction of the canal began. By that time work was also under way at Gloucester on the Herefordshire and Gloucestershire canal. That canal reached Ledbury in 1798 but it

added little to the city's trade in coal and agricultural produce. Work on the Gloucester and Berkeley canal ground to a halt in 1799 and interest in the project only revived in 1811 when a tramroad linking Gloucester and Cheltenham was completed. From 1812 vessels were able to enter the basin from the river through a double lock downstream of the city quay, and the basin shared in a thriving trade in coal from the Forest of Dean and from traditional sources in the West Midlands and South Wales. Traffic on the tramroad, which served both quay and basin, also included stone destined for Cheltenham and in 1824 an arm was built on the side of the canal south of the basin for barges participating in the coal and stone trades. With the completion of the canal in 1827 there was an immediate and dramatic increase in Gloucester's sea-going trade. The city became a busy port handling corn and timber imports bound for Birmingham and other parts of the West Midlands. Gloucester's prosperity as a port stimulated commercial and industrial activity in the city and was consolidated by the new railways, beginning with a line to Birmingham opened in 1840. Its position on major land routes made Gloucester an important railway town and in the 1840s and '50s it also obtained railway links with Bristol, London and South Wales.

In the mid-19th century commercial and industrial development centred on the area around the canal basin and the head of the canal next to the Bristol road. Additional wharves were constructed, warehouses and factories were built, timber yards were laid out, and an elaborate network of railway sidings was created. The first large warehouses, a pair on the north side of the basin, were built by the canal company in 1827. Later warehouses around the basin were built by corn merchants in a distinctive style determined by the company and their survival has contributed much to the character and fame of Gloucester. The docks area was enlarged in 1849 when a new basin, known as the Victoria or Southgate dock, opened on the east side of the main basin. The new wharves included Baker's quay on the east side of the canal below Llanthony bridge. Named after Samuel Baker, a West

3 For many centuries traffic on the river Severn played an important rôle in Gloucester's trade. In this view from the south-west, in the mid 18th century, a ship passes the Naight, a small island, to join other vessels at the city quay and conical glasshouses on the west side of the city provide the only sign of industrial activity. Other buildings shown include, from left to right, Eagle Hall (the Duke of Norfolk's House), the top of St Mary de Lode tower, St Nicholas's spire, the county gaol (the castle keep), Marybone House, the cathedral, Holy Trinity tower (a clock tower), St John's spire, St Michael's tower, Blackfriars and St Mary de Crypt tower. The river channel east of the Naight was to be closed during the construction of the canal basin to form a double lock for vessels passing between the river and the basin.

Indies merchant from Bristol, the quay was completed in 1840 and High Orchard, the area behind it, was quickly filled with industrial buildings and yards. That area had been the orchard of Llanthony Priory, a religious house dissolved by Henry VIII. Llanthony quay, west of the canal next to the priory's surviving buildings on the Hempsted road, was finished by the Great Western Railway in 1854 to handle exports of Forest of Dean coal.

The docks soon supplanted the city quay as the centre of commercial activity and in 1845 a new custom house was built near the main basin. The docks' heyday was, however, short. Gloucester's advantages as an inland port were offset by the inability of larger vessels to use the canal and many cargoes bound for the city were transferred to lighters at the canal entrance at Sharpness. The development of a more comprehensive railway network to the Midlands worked to the advantage of other ports and after the early 1860s investment in major capital projects in Gloucester's docks became less frequent. In the mid 1870s the canal company built new docks at Sharpness but within a few years it faced competition from new docks lower down the Severn estuary at Avonmouth and Portishead.

In the mid-19th century Gloucester's economy supported a great variety of trades and crafts and its cattle market, held from 1823 on the east side of the city, thrived. A small but growing number of foundries worked iron from the Forest of Dean and the success of new industries more than compensated for the decline of pinmaking and other traditional industries. With the growth in water-borne commerce several boat yards were opened and a number of related industries, notably the making of sails, ropes, and sacks, started. The port's staple imports, grain and timber, stimulated much industrial activity. Gloucester became an important centre for flour milling and its malting industry expanded. Timber was supplied to the building trades and to furniture makers, several of whom started their businesses in the mid-19th century. Match making was introduced in 1867 and Gloucester became closely associated with the industry through the enterprise of S.J. Moreland, who registered the England's Glory label as his trademark in 1891.

In the later 19th century Gloucester prospered as an industrial and manufacturing town. Foundry work increased and several successful engineering firms were established. Manufacturing production also diversified with the establishment of businesses making goods such as pickles and vinegar, shirts, hairpins, toys and folding furniture. The city's economic fortunes were exemplified by the progress of the wagon works built in 1860 to make and repair railway trucks. Production later also included railway carriages and road vehicles. In 1897 the company, with 1,100 employees, was the largest firm in Gloucester. Fielding & Platt, the principal engineering firm and a specialist in hydraulic machinery and oil and gas engines, employed 500 people at that time. Trade at the docks continued to grow in the late 19th and early 20th centuries. Most of the increase in traffic was accounted for by timber imports and in 1891 the docks company built a new dock west of the canal in Monk Meadow, some way below Llanthony bridge, for the trade.

From the 1820s brick and stucco fronts continued to be added to buildings in the main streets of the old city and by 1850 most of the remaining timber fronts had disappeared and the streets included large shop windows. In the same period several new roads were built just outside the city centre. To the north Worcester Street, leading off Northgate Street, was laid out in 1822 and replaced Hare Lane as the main road to Tewkesbury. To the east Clarence Street, laid out in 1832 and 1833 from the city end of Barton Street to the new cattle market, became the main road to the two railway stations opened next to the cattle market in the early 1840s. The stations were also reached from Northgate Street along St Aldate Street but the entrance to that route was steep and narrow and in 1851 an

4 Gloucester castle was built by Walter of Gloucester, sheriff of Gloucestershire, in the early 12th century on a site on the south-west side of the town overlooking the river Severn. It replaced an earlier Norman fortification and was enlarged several times. Few additions were made after the 1260s and its buildings and defences were demolished piecemeal from 1498. The keep, which became the county gaol, remained standing until 1787 when it was pulled down to make way for a new prison.

alternative route, later called George Street, was built further down Northgate Street. On the south side of the city Kimbrose Lane, an old narrow street leading off Southgate Street, was replaced in 1847 by Commercial Road as the main road to the docks. Traffic movement in the old city was also improved by the demolition of protruding buildings and other obstacles and at the Cross congestion was eased by the rebuilding of the nave of St Michael's church on a new alignment in 1849. In the mid-1850s Priory Road was built along the course of Dockham ditch between lower Westgate Street and St Catherine Street to reduce the number of vehicles passing through the city centre.

In the later 19th century the basically Georgian character of the main streets was modified by new public buildings and commercial premises. Among the more imposing street fronts were the porticos of the Southgate Street corn exchange and the Eastgate Street produce market, built in 1856 on the sites of the markets opened in 1786, and the long façade of the *Bell* hotel in Southgate Street, refronted during alterations begun in 1864. Nonconformist chapels in lower Southgate Street and lower Northgate Street were rebuilt on a grander scale, and in Brunswick Road, leading off Eastgate Street, the Baptist chapel was rebuilt twice and, on the opposite side of the street, an impressive building was completed for the Schools of Science and Art in 1872. Among the new shops of the period were stores built for a local co-operative society on the corners of Brunswick Road with Eastgate Street and Barton Street in 1867 and 1877. The pace of building quickened at the end of the century and new public buildings, banks and shops had transformed the appearance of the city centre by the First World War. The most prominent new buildings were in Eastgate Street, where the Guildhall was completed in 1892 and imposing premises were provided for the National Provincial Bank and Lloyds Bank in 1888 and 1898 respectively. At the Cross the Tolsey, having been replaced as the city offices by the Guildhall, was pulled down and its site on the corner of Southgate and Westgate Streets was filled in 1895 with a new building for the Wilts and Dorset Banking Company. Three shops on the corner of Northgate and Westgate Streets were replaced in 1907 by a new building for the London City and Midland Bank. In Brunswick Road new buildings were completed next to the Schools of Science and Art for the Price Memorial Hall and a public library in 1893 and 1900 respectively. Many street improvements were carried out and in 1892 and 1893 College Street, leading off Westgate Street, was widened to form a ceremonial approach to the cathedral. The major road project of the period, completed in 1913, was the widening of the section of lower Westgate Street above the Island.

Although the city's population rose from 7,597 to 8,280 in the first decade of the 19th century, Gloucester did not begin to grow until the last years of the Napoleonic Wars. The first new suburb grew up at a spa opened in 1815 south of the city and, known as the Spa, comprised fashionable houses. Later suburbs were for Gloucester's new industrial classes and, as the proximity of the river Severn and its floodlands prevented building west of the city and north of Kingsholm, they were confined mainly to the south and east. Low-lying land was filled piecemeal with closely packed streets of artisan dwellings, usually of two storeys, and higher ground was used for more spacious houses for the middle classes. The new houses were of brick made in the meadows by the Severn. After 1835, when the city was enlarged to take in the Spa and an additional part of Barton Street, Gloucester grew more rapidly but it failed to regain its place as Gloucestershire's largest town, a position recently usurped by Cheltenham. Whereas most of the artisan houses built in the 1820s and the early 1830s were on the north-east side of the city in the Alvin Street area, most building in the mid-19th century took place on the south-east in the Barton Street and Tredworth suburbs and on the south adjoining the Bristol and Stroud roads. By the 1860s many of Gloucester's residents lived in streets outside the city boundary and in 1871 the city, the municipal borough, had a population of 18,341 whereas the larger parliamentary borough had a population of 31,844. In 1874 the city was enlarged to cover the same area as the parliamentary borough by the addition of Kingsholm to the north, part of Wotton to the east, the outer Barton Street and Tredworth areas to the south-east, and parts of the Bristol and Stroud roads to the south. The corporation's decision to levy higher rates in those areas to pay for services such as sewerage and mains water inadvertently encouraged building beyond the new boundary and in 1900 the city's area was again increased to include suburbs in the Coney Hill, Saintbridge, Tuffley, and Bristol road areas to the south-east and south as well as land on the west side of the canal below Llanthony bridge. The city's population, 47,955 in 1901, was over six times what it had been a century earlier and it exceeded 50,000 before the start of the First World War in 1914.

In the early 19th century Gloucester's administration was dominated by the city corporation and particularly by the aldermen in their rôle as the city's magistrates. The corporation, whose powers derived from the charter of 1483, was a closed body and by the early 19th century professional men, notably lawyers and surgeons, had a disproportionate influence over it compared with tradesmen. Although other citizens were involved in government through bodies responsible for poor relief and street improvements and lighting, the exclusion of some prominent citizens from the main governing body caused ill feeling.

5 At the beginning of the 19th century Gloucester was not much larger than the area once protected by its medieval walls. The main suburb in the fields and orchards beyond was Barton Street. The new canal basin was not yet in use and the canal to Berkeley was unfinished. On this map of 1805 two coats of arms, that granted to the town in 1538 and that adopted by the corporation in 1647, are displayed to the left and right respectively of the arms of Gloucester diocese.

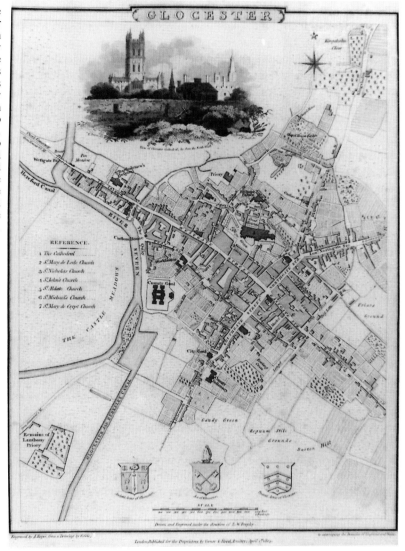

Corruption and other evils associated with the closed system of government were not as prevalent in Gloucester as elsewhere and in the early 1830s the main criticisms levelled against the corporation were its undue influence in parliamentary elections, a long-standing complaint, and lethargy in some areas of administration.

In 1835 the ruling oligarchy was replaced by an elected council. The new council, chosen on a limited franchise, made few significant changes in civic matters and many officials retained their positions. At first the reformed corporation's rôle in government was small, its main task being to establish a police force and maintain law and order. Many services were outside its control and poor relief in the city was administered from 1835 by the board of guardians of the new Gloucester union. As part of the reforms initiated in 1835 charities and several almshouses administered by the old corporation came under the control of appointed trustees and the city magistracy also became independent of the corporation.

In the early 19th century many parts of Gloucester developed into slums with polluted water supplies. Conditions were particularly insanitary in the older western districts near the river where once fashionable houses were converted as lodgings and their back yards were filled with cottages and where flooding was an occasional hazard when the Severn over-flowed its banks. Although public health became an issue in the city in 1831, during the first great cholera epidemic of the 19th century, little was done to improve sanitary conditions in the city until 1847, when cholera again threatened. In 1849, on its creation as the board of health for the city, the corporation acquired more effective powers to deal with nuisances and a few years later it embarked on two major projects, the construction of a sewerage and drainage system and the improvement of the water supply. Those initiatives were too late to prevent the return of cholera in 1849 and 1854. Conditions were even more squalid in the suburbs outside the city where parish government was impotent to control speculative building. Local boards of health attempted to deal with nuisances in the Barton Street and Kingsholm areas from the mid 1860s but effective measures were possible only from 1874 when those suburbs became part of the city.

In the late 19th and early 20th centuries the work of the council increased as the corporation acquired additional responsibilities in matters such as public health and provided a greater range of services. Piecemeal slum clearance began in 1909 and the first council houses were built in 1919. The city's tram system, established in 1879, was run privately until 1902 when it was purchased by the corporation, converted to electric traction, and extended beyond the city boundary to reach the village of Hucclecote to the east. The municipal electricity works had been opened in 1900. An elected school board, formed in 1876, built four elementary schools in the city and the corporation, which in the late 19th century became involved in running secondary and technical schools, took over the board's schools in 1903 when it became the local education authority.

In the 19th century Gloucester's cultural life was influenced by the numerical predominance of its working-class population and communities. Although fashionable society had largely abandoned the city for the neighbouring spa town of Cheltenham, Gloucester, as the county town, remained the home of important county institutions, including from 1823 a lunatic asylum, and associations and some gentry families continued to figure in city life. At the beginning of Victoria's reign the influence of the cathedral clergy in city life was at a low ebb. The cathedral's status had been diminished in 1836 when the diocese was merged with that of Bristol and the bishop, James Monk, left Gloucester, and the non-resident dean, Edward Rice, took little interest in cathedral affairs. The appointment in 1862 of Henry Law as dean infused new vigour in the life of the cathedral clergy and laity. A few years earlier a new bishop, Charles Baring, had returned to the bishop's palace. The union of the sees lasted until 1897. Every third year the cathedral was the main setting for the Three Choirs' Festival, which had grown out of the annual meeting, established by 1718, of the cathedral choirs of Gloucester, Hereford and Worcester. The Gloucester festival, which was patronised by the local gentry, grew in popularity in the early 19th century and the railways brought even larger crowds to the city for it. The Shire Hall assembly room, the city's principal concert hall, was also used for the festival.

Gloucester with its staunch Protestant tradition, established during the 16th-century Reformation, was a bastion of evangelical religion in the following centuries. George Whitefield, born in the city in 1714, became famous throughout the country as one of the greatest preachers of his day and the Sunday School movement began in Gloucester in 1780 through the efforts of local newspaper owner, Robert Raikes, in collaboration with the

Rev. Thomas Stock, master of the cathedral school. In the 19th century Anglicans and Protestant nonconformists built churches and chapels in the expanding city and its suburbs. Of the nonconformists the Baptists, the Independents, and the various Methodist churches attracted the largest congregations and a religious census conducted by the *Gloucester Journal* newspaper in 1881 revealed that more people attended nonconformist chapels than Anglican churches. The small Roman Catholic community grew and in 1859 rebuilt its church. A few years later Gloucester's Protestant heritage was recalled by the erection of an imposing memorial to John Hooper, Bishop of Gloucester, on the spot outside the cathedral precinct in St Mary's Square where Hooper had been burned at the stake in 1555. A small Jewish community established in the mid-18th century had a synagogue and a cemetery in Barton Street. Its later synagogue, in lower Southgate Street, closed in the mid-19th century and the community had dispersed by the end of the century.

In the mid-19th century local philanthropists, many of them evangelical Christians, attempted to alleviate the problems of crime, drunkenness, and prostitution. Seamen and boatmen frequenting the docks became the targets of missionaries, some of whom may have shared the town clerk's opinion in 1836 that the growth in the port's trade had led to a rise in crime. For one mission, supported by the Church of England, a chapel was built in the docks in 1849. For a few years from 1878 Norwegian seamen employed in the timber trade were able to worship in a small wooden chapel built alongside the canal at the wagon works. Gloucester's clergy took a prominent place in missionary and philanthropic ventures. Typical was Thomas Hedley, who in 1841 became the first minister of St James's church in the Barton Street suburb and in 1844 built a school for his parishioners' children. More exceptional was Samuel Lysons, who in 1834 inherited the Hempsted Court estate south of the city near the docks and the Bristol road. His concern for the welfare of his less exalted neighbours led him to build a church and a school there as well as several houses. The church, at High Orchard, was dedicated to St Luke in 1841 and Lysons was its minister until 1866 when he resigned, disillusioned by the apparent failure of his mission.

The energies of Gloucester's citizens were channelled into a variety of political and educational institutions and, apart from ubiquitous public houses, their need for entertainment and recreation was met in a number of venues. Places of entertainment, which included a theatre built in 1791 in Westgate Street, proliferated with the opening of music halls and picture houses or cinemas. Sporting activity blossomed after Gloucester Park was opened in 1862. The spa grounds, which formed part of the park, were used by many sports clubs in the later 19th century. Among them was Gloucester Football Club, formed in 1873 to play rugby union football. In 1891 it moved to a new ground at Kingsholm, where it has become the chief standard bearer of Gloucester's sporting tradition.

Change in the 20th Century

After the First World War manufacturing and engineering industries continued to provide many jobs and from the late 1920s, when the Gloster Aircraft Company switched production from Cheltenham to a new factory on a wartime airfield at Hucclecote, Gloucester was closely associated with the aircraft industry. That industry benefited from the re-armament programme begun in the later 1930s and the Gloster company, which built a second factory at Brockworth, produced many fighter aircraft during the Second World War. Although Gloucester remained an important timber port, trade at the docks was in decline by the 1930s as the canal faced increasing competition from road transport. In the later 20th century established industries including engineering and flour milling also declined. Aircraft production ceased in 1960. Moreland's match factory closed in 1976 and the wagon works, where production had turned to freight containers, tractors, and loading trucks, closed in the mid-1980s. Some new manufacturing industries were established but employment increasingly depended on service industries such as banking and retailing and on jobs in local government and health services.

The city's railway network was drastically reduced in the 1960s and '70s and passenger traffic was served by a single station from 1975. Gloucester remained an important centre for road transport and the construction of new roads on its fringes attracted businesses to the area and had a major influence on the city's physical development. A bypass road for traffic between South Wales and Bristol, running from Westgate bridge and north and east of the city, was begun in the early 1930s and completed in 1958 when the section between the Stroud road at Tuffley and the Bristol road north of Quedgeley was opened. East of the city the Barnwood bypass, running from the city bypass and north of Barnwood and Hucclecote, was completed in 1966. Later new roads were built to link Gloucester with the Bristol-Birmingham motorway, which opened east of the city in 1971, and in 1983 an outer northern bypass, crossing the Severn's eastern channel to a junction with the Chepstow and Ledbury roads, was completed.

In the 1920s and '30s the inner part of Gloucester changed considerably. The appearance of the central streets, particularly Northgate and Eastgate Streets, was altered by new shops and several areas of slum dwellings were demolished. In the largest clearance the Oxbode, leading off Northgate Street, and King's Square were formed between 1927 and 1929 for commercial development. In the 1950s and '60s slum-clearance schemes transformed the lower Westgate Street and Alvin Street areas and later several 19th-century suburban streets were the subject of housing improvement schemes. Some areas remained liable to flooding after one of the greatest ever floods of the river Severn inundated large parts of the city in 1947.

In the later 20th century much redevelopment in the city centre was designed to reduce traffic congestion and many buildings, including some of historic or architectural interest, were demolished. At the Cross the entrance to Eastgate Street was widened by the demolition, completed in 1956, of the nave of St Michael's church. Traffic ignoring the bypass road added to the city's problems until a ban on through traffic brought immediate relief to the city centre. Long-distance traffic disappeared from the city with the opening of the Severn Road bridge in 1966 and the Bristol-Birmingham motorway in 1971. The first sections of an inner ring road around the centre were completed in 1962. The road joined the bypass near Westgate bridge, which remained an obstacle to traffic until the early 1970s when it was replaced by a pair of bridges forming part of a new western approach road.

In the city centre work began in the later 1960s on two pedestrian shopping precincts with car parking at roof level linked by bridges over Eastgate Street and Southgate Street. Those projects, the King's Walk centre, which incorporated King's Square, and the Eastgate centre completed in 1972 and 1974 respectively, involved the closure of old streets and the demolition of many buildings. A pedestrian way called the Via Sacra was created using some ancient streets to link the new shopping precincts with the cathedral and other historic buildings. Further pedestrianisation of the city centre occurred in the early 1990s when Eastgate Street and the upper part of Westgate Street were closed to traffic, and in 1994 the bridge over Southgate Street was removed, thereby restoring the view along the street. In the docks the area around the main basin fell into decay after the Second World War and some warehouses were demolished. In a move spearheaded by the city council the area was redeveloped from the late 1970s for commercial and leisure use. Many smaller buildings were demolished, surviving warehouses were adapted for use as offices, museums, and other leisure facilities, and a number of shops and restaurants were built.

In the 20th century large tracts of farmland to the south and east of Gloucester were covered with suburban houses. The city corporation built several estates, including many houses in the Linden Road and Tuffley areas to the south, immediately after the First World War, and in the late 1920s or early '30s large council estates were built at Finlay Road and Coney Hill to the south-east for people displaced by slum clearance in the older part of the city. Most private houses built before the Second World War were in the Cheltenham road area to the north-east and particularly at Longlevens, which took its name from the Long Elevens, strips of land once part of a common field north of the Longford road. Suburban development after the Second World War was on a huge scale. Large council estates were begun at Podsmead and Lower Tuffley to the south and at Elmbridge to the north-east in the late 1940s and at Matson to the south-east in the early 1950s. From the 1970s large private estates were built on the outskirts of the city and by the end of the century the suburbs extended into the ancient parishes of Barnwood, Churchdown and Brockworth to the east, Matson and Upton St Leonards to the south-east, and Hempsted, Quedgeley and Hardwicke to the south-west and a number of outlying villages, including Hucclecote, were engulfed by housing estates.

Gloucester's growth was marked by several extensions of the city boundary in the mid-20th century. The first extension, in 1935, doubled the city's area by adding land on the east at Wotton and Coney Hill and on the south at Matson, Tuffley, Lower Tuffley and Podsmead. There were further boundary changes in 1951 and 1957, and in 1967 the city absorbed suburbs at Longlevens and Innsworth to the north-east, Barnwood and Hucclecote to the east, and Hempsted to the south-west. In the 1970s and '80s land within the new boundary, which on the south-east followed the Bristol-Birmingham motorway, was filled with new housing estates. Robins Wood Hill, in the south between Matson and Tuffley, was left as a place of recreation. The inclusion in the city of land at Sneedham's Green to the south-east and the Quedgeley suburb to the south-west in 1991 increased its population to over 100,000. The city corporation's powers and involvement in city life were reduced after the Second World War and in 1974 the city relinquished its status as a county borough, a status it had enjoyed since 1889.

The changes of the later 20th century had a dramatic impact on Gloucester. Many older parts of the city were transformed in appearance but much survived to reveal Gloucester's rich and diverse heritage. The cathedral or former abbey church, its 15th-century central tower a landmark in the surrounding countryside, and the docks with their collection of mid-19th-century warehouses were its chief tourist attractions. With the arrival of people from new Commonwealth countries some of the 19th-century suburbs, particularly the Barton Street and Tredworth areas, became home to ethnic communities with their own clubs and churches or mosques.

Quay and Docks

6   This view of 1850 southwards from the city quay towards the docks includes the track of the Gloucester and Cheltenham tramroad along the river bank behind the county gaol and the entrance to the double lock between the river and the dock basin. The warehouse alongside the lock was built by the Birmingham corn merchants Joseph and Charles Sturge in 1834 and the more distant chimney was attached to an engine house pumping water from the river to the basin.

7   This photograph of Gloucester docks was taken from the north quay in 1883. The vessels in the main basin include sailing ships, canal boats, timber lighters, and trows, the last being flat-bottomed boats traditionally employed in Gloucester's river trade. *Dr. Witte*, the brig in the centre, had brought wheat from the Baltic port of Rostock.

8 In the late 19th century horses were used in the docks for hauling railway wagons and stone provided ballast for sea-going vessels leaving Gloucester. This view from the north quay *c*.1887 shows three warehouses, Phillpotts, Kimberley and Herbert, built on the east side of the main basin in 1846. Behind Fox's petroleum stores, built in 1882, is Albert Mills, a flour mill established in a warehouse on the west side of the Victoria dock in 1869.

9 The growth in corn imports following the repeal of the Corn Laws in 1846 encouraged growth in the flour industry in Gloucester. City Mills, the first of eight new flour mills opened by the 1870s, was built in the docks in 1850 by Joseph and Jonah Hadley and was operated from 1886 by a partnership between Charles Priday, F.K.S. Metford, and F.T. Pearce. With the closure of Albert Mills in 1977, City Mills was the only flour mill in the city until it too closed in 1994.

10 This photograph shows a brigantine moored at the west quay *c*.1905. The buildings were part of a range of eight warehouses built between 1829 and 1831 to a uniform design provided by the Birmingham corn merchants Joseph and Charles Sturge. From *c*.1869 the end warehouse, on the left, was used as a flour mill, named St Owen's Mills after the parish which included most of the docks area. The buildings were demolished in 1966.

11 In the late 19th century corn was unloaded manually by gangs of dockers, who packed it into sacks before transferring it to warehouses or directly to canal boats. The main sack-hiring firm was founded by salt merchant Gopsill Brown (d.1867). This group of porters also used sacks owned by Healing & Sons, a family business operating a flour mill up river in Tewkesbury.

12 Together with grain, timber was a staple of the port's trade well into the 20th century. Much wood was imported as deals, pieces sawn to a standard size, and in this scene of *c*.1935 men are unloading a lighter in the barge arm.

13 The main timber yards in the later 19th century were on the east side of the canal in the Bristol road area. In the 1890s the docks company provided additional facilities for timber importers on the west side in Monk Meadow. This view, taken before 1904, looks north-westwards to the shallow pond or timber float excavated in Monk Meadow in 1896. Monk Meadow dock, further along the canal towards Llanthony bridge, was opened in 1892.

14 Salt from Droitwich and Stoke Prior in Worcestershire provided the docks' only regular export. The Victoria dock, opened in 1849, became the main centre for the trade and salt brought by canal and rail was transhipped on its east side. This view of the dock, looking north-westwards and postmarked 1911, includes canal boats belonging to the Stoke Prior works and the Gloucester coal merchants and carriers Jacob Rice & Son.

15 (*right*) In 1867 the brig *Ada* brought linseed from the Black Sea port of Taganrog to Foster Brothers' oil and cake mill on the south end of Baker's quay. The mill was built in 1863 and Pillar Warehouse on the north end of the quay in 1838. This view northwards also shows Llanthony quay, where the coal-handling equipment was dismantled in 1869, and Great Western Warehouse, built north of Llanthony Road in 1863.

16 (*above*) In the early 20th century many goods imported through Gloucester docks for the Midlands were carried from Bristol Channel ports by the Severn & Canal Carrying Co. Formed in 1873 by a merger of Worcester and Stourport firms, the company transhipped cargoes to canal boats at Gloucester, where it occupied two warehouses beside the barge arm.

17 The mariners' chapel, opened in the docks in 1849, was built by private benefactors for a mission to seamen and boatmen visiting the docks. It was supported by the established church and services were occasionally conducted in foreign languages. The chaplain also held services on boats and here the chaplain in 1914, the Rev. William Henry Whalley, is seen with his helpers and a portable harmonium.

18 This view northwards from the canal lock to the city quay shows the slipways provided in the late 1880s when the quay was extended over the river foreshore. The front of the old custom house was erected in 1724 but the building dates from 1581, the year after the city obtained the status of a port. On the right, the river wall behind the prison was constructed in 1937, when the road there became a bypass for traffic avoiding the city centre, and the warders' cottages at the corner of the prison were built in 1921.

Trade and Industry

19 Barton Fair originated in a grant of 1465 under which the abbot of Gloucester held a three-day fair on the feast of St Lambert (17 September) outside the town in Barton Street. It was an important cheese fair in the 18th century when it took place on one day, 28 September after the calendar change of 1752. Later mops or hiring fairs were held on several Mondays following it. Barton Fair became Gloucester's chief pleasure fair and in 1823, when it was acquired by the city corporation, livestock sales were moved to the new cattle market. The pleasure fair continued to be held in Barton Street and, as this photograph of 1882 shows, stalls extended along Eastgate Street. In 1904 the fair moved to Oxlease, on Alney Island west of the city.

20 The river Twyver, a tributary stream of the Severn, powered at least five mills along its course between Saintbridge and Barton Street, east of Gloucester. Brown's Mill, at the east end of India Road, was recorded from 1540 and was a corn mill in the late 19th century. It ceased operating in *c*.1910. In the 1740s it had been a cloth mill and in the 1820s and '30s it had been occupied by a firm of edgetool makers.

21 Among industries which thrived in Gloucester in the later 17th century was glassmaking. This building, demolished in 1933, was the remains of a large conical glasshouse built in 1694. It stood by the river Severn near the north end of the city quay.

22 In 1823 the corporation opened a new cattle market. Until then livestock sales had been conducted in various streets, including those leading off St Mary's Square west of the cathedral. The new market, south of lower Northgate Street, was an open space enclosed by a wall and planted with plane trees. The market's trade increased following the building of railways next to it and it became an important source of revenue for the corporation. It was enlarged several times, an 1899 extension taking the boundary as far as George Street.

23 Livestock auctions were first held in the cattle market in 1862 by the partnership of Henry Bruton and William Knowles. They founded a well-known firm of auctioneers and estate agents, which later shared the market business with the firm of . Pearce Pope and Sons. The cattle market moved to a new site in St Oswald's Road, on the city's outskirts, between 1955 and 1958 and a bus station opened on the abandoned site in 1962.

24 Gloucester's wagon works in Bristol Road next to the canal were built in 1860 by the Gloucester Wagon Co., a local business founded to make, repair, and hire railway trucks. The factory was enlarged several times, notably in 1875 when it took over joinery works next to it, and production was diversified to include railway carriages. The company, known from 1888 as the Gloucester Railway Carriage & Wagon Co., became the largest employer in Gloucester with a workforce of over 1,100 people at the end of the century.

25 The wagon works' offices in Bristol Road, shown here, faced the entrance to Stroud Road and were pulled down in 1904 to make way for a grander company building.

26 Between 1893, when they took over carriage and wheel works in Ladybellgate Street from Mousell Brothers, and 1908 the wagon works' owners also made road vehicles. In 1894 they built a showroom for their new products in George Street. It was sold in 1904 to the Post Office for an extension of its premises near the G.W.R. station.

27 This showroom, opened in 1898, stood on the cattle market side of George Street and was the second to be built by the wagon company for its road vehicles. In 1923 it was converted for use as a corn exchange but by the late 1930s it had become a popular dance hall, called Prince's Hall.

28 The engineering business established by Samuel Fielding and James Platt at the Atlas ironworks at High Orchard in the late 1860s became a leading employer in the city. This scene in front of the works, in St Luke's Street, includes a dray owned by the Midland Railway.

29 Samuel John Moreland built his match factory in Bristol Road in 1868. In its early days he stored wood in a timber float on the canal at Two Mile Bend between Hemsted and Quedgeley and employed many women and children as outworkers making matchboxes. The idea for his England's Glory trademark, adopted in 1891, came from a label produced by Thomas Gee, owner of a match factory in the Island in the early 1870s.

30 Moreland's factory, which had 640 workers in 1907, was enlarged in 1911. Moreland's sons Harry and Philip joined the business and here Harry is pictured, second from the right, in the factory's main match-making room. The Moreland family continued to run the business after it was acquired by Bryant & May in 1913 and until 1972. The factory closed in 1976.

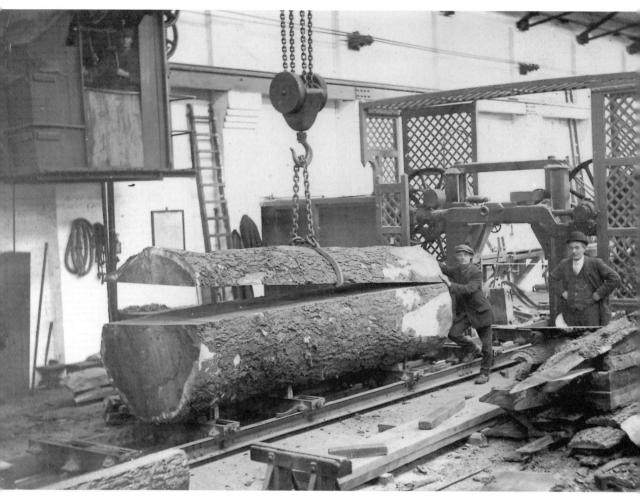

31 The most successful timber business in Gloucester was established by Morgan Price (d.1776), who imported deals from the Baltic. The business, continued by his descendants and known from 1889 as Price, Walker & Co., dominated the city's timber trade in the later 19th century. The company, which imported logs as well as deals, employed up to 700 people at its Gloucester yard and mills in Bristol Road in 1904 and remained independent until 1962.

32 In the late 19th century several hundred men worked in the printing industry. John Jennings, who started his business in Bell Lane in 1876 and built a factory (shown here in 1911) in Brunswick Road in 1883, had 30 employees in 1897. Larger printing businesses included that established in 1858 by the writer and Quaker John Bellows, who employed 100 men in 1897.

33 Gloucester's most successful furniture-making business was established by John Albert Matthews in 1863. His first premises were at the corner of Southgate Street and Parliament Street and in 1897 he built a large factory at High Orchard. He then employed 200 people. The factory was completely destroyed on 23 July 1912 in one of Gloucester's biggest fires.

34 In the later 19th century a number of Gloucester's new businesses including clothing, pickle and jam, and toy companies provided jobs for large numbers of women. One was the shirt factory in Magdala Road. Built in 1887, it had 170 employees in 1897.

35 In 1870 John Stephens opened a pickle and vinegar factory at the north end of Hare Lane. The factory, which also made jam from 1893, was enlarged and in 1897 it had 400 employees, mostly women. During a strike in 1912 a leading trade unionist Abel Joseph Evans (pictured centre) attempted mediation between the factory manager and workers. Evans, who had been the local secretary of the dockers' union, was also a city councillor, having been first elected to the council in 1896.

The Cathedral

36 When Gloucester diocese was created in 1541 the former abbey church of St Peter became its cathedral. The abbey had originated as a minster, which was founded in the later seventh century and became a Benedictine house in 1022, and had been dissolved in 1540. The large Romanesque church dates from a rebuilding begun by Abbot Serlo in 1086 and the nave had been completed by 1122.

37 John Thoky, abbot of Gloucester, brought the body of Edward II, murdered at Berkeley castle in 1327, to the abbey church for burial. The tomb, on the north side of the presbytery, quickly became a shrine and offerings by pilgrims from all over England helped to pay for building work at the church in the mid-14th century.

38 Building work at the abbey in the 14th century during which the south transept and the choir were remodelled had considerable influence on the development of the English perpendicular style. This view from the south-east also shows two major architectural achievements of the 15th century, the great central tower of the 1450s and the later lady chapel.

39 The great cloister on the north side of the cathedral church dates from a rebuilding of the later 14th century. The fan vault is even more elaborate than that which the monks and their masons had used for the richly decorated choir of the church.

40 The imposing south porch built by John Morwent, abbot of Gloucester 1420-37, and other parts of the cathedral were stripped of much of their ornamentation during the Reformation. As part of a restoration begun in 1868 by the architect George Gilbert Scott, the porch's fabric was renewed, a sundial which had been inserted on its south front was removed, and new figures placed in the niches. The statue of Queen Anne, left of the porch in College Green, the main part of the cathedral close, was carved in 1711 or 1712 and stood in that position between 1838 and 1865.

41 St Mary's gate was the principal entrance to Gloucester Abbey in the Middle Ages. Built in the 12th century at the centre of the abbey's west wall, it took its name from the church of St Mary de Lode standing nearby outside the abbey precinct (later the cathedral close).

42 Miller's Green, the inner court of the cathedral close, was called Palace Yard in the 19th century. It includes a group of medieval buildings at the north-west corner of the church. Among them is a range, the lower storey of which dates from the 13th century. The later timber-framed upper storey has become known as the Parliament Room, recalling the time parliament met in the abbey in 1378. The range may have been part of a longer building where early kings are thought to have held their councils or parliaments. The tall brick house to the left was one of several built in the close in the late 17th century.

43 Charles John Ellicott (1819-1905) was bishop of Gloucester and Bristol from 1863 and of Gloucester alone from 1897 when the union of the sees of 1836 was dissolved. Taking up residence in 1863 in the new bishop's palace in the cathedral close, he opened a theological college in Gloucester in 1869 but it lapsed before the end of his episcopate. That lasted until 1905 when he retired because of age and infirmity.

Religious Houses

44 St Oswald's Priory originated as a minster church founded north of Gloucester *c*.900 by Ethelfleda of Mercia. The relics of St Oswald, king of Northumbria, were translated to it in 909. It became an Augustinian priory in the mid-12th century. After the priory's dissolution in 1536 the north transept and aisle of its church became the parish church of St Catherine. Most of the other buildings were demolished and St Catherine's church was pulled down in the mid-1650s.

45 Llanthony Priory, properly called Llanthony Secunda, was established south-west of Gloucester in 1137 for Augustinian canons from a house in Wales. It was dissolved in 1539 and its surviving buildings were used as a farmstead in the 18th and 19th centuries. The stone range with the timber-framed upper storey dates from the late Middle Ages.

46   Some buildings of Llanthony Priory were destroyed at the siege of Gloucester in 1643, when the royalists used the site as a battery, and the priory church had been demolished by the 18th century. The Gloucester and Berkeley canal crosses the east side of the priory precinct and the ruined late-medieval gatehouse, pictured here, stands on the west side by the road to Hempsted.

47   In the mid-13th century Franciscan, Dominican and Carmelite friaries were founded in Gloucester. The Franciscan house, Greyfriars, was built to the east of Southgate Street. It was dissolved in 1538 and the site passed into private ownership in 1544. Many of the friary buildings, including part of its early 16th-century church, had disappeared by the early 18th century. Several substantial houses were built on the site and, in the mid-18th century, dwellings were built within the remains of the church. In this view of *c*.1800 St Mary de Crypt church is in the background.

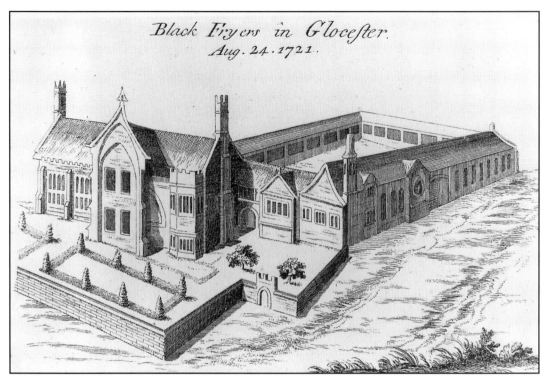

48 The Dominican friary, Blackfriars, was to the west of Southgate Street on a site north of the town wall. It was sold in 1539 to Thomas Bell, a wealthy capper and clothier, who converted the mid-13th-century friary church as a house (shown here, in 1721, on the left) and used buildings around the cloister for business. Other dwellings were formed there later and parts of the buildings were used for industry until the mid-20th century.

49 In 1876 Thomas Gambier Parry of Highnam moved St Lucy's Home of Charity, which he had founded in 1864 for a community of nursing sisters, from the Tewkesbury road to College Gardens at the corner of Hare Lane and Pitt Street. There it adjoined the outpatients' department of the children's hospital, which like the home was run by the Clewer sisters of St John the Baptist. The new home included a chapel, which became the main centre of Anglo-Catholic ritual in the city. The home closed in 1933.

Churches and Chapels

50 St Michael's church, at the Cross on the north side of Eastgate Street, was one of Gloucester's medieval parish churches. The west tower, added between 1455 and 1472, was retained in 1849, when the church was rebuilt on a larger scale and on a different alignment to allow the street to be widened, and was preserved in 1955, when the church was demolished. This photograph of 1904 or 1905 also shows the building erected for the Gloucestershire Banking Co. in the late 1830s and, next to it, the Eastgate market portico of 1856.

51 St Aldate's church, opened in 1756, served a parish which had been without a place of worship since the demolition of its medieval church in the mid-1650s. The new church, on or near the site of its predecessor in St Aldate Street, was a simple brick building with a bellcot. Of the fittings the pulpit and bell came from a chapel which the city corporation had opened in Tolsey in 1738. After closure in the 1931, St Aldate's church was used as a hall until its demolition in 1963.

52 St Catherine's church, Priory Road, was consecrated in 1868. It stood next to the ruins of St Oswald's Priory, part of which had served as a parish church until the mid-1650s. One of the city's M.P.s, Charles James Monk, who as a child had lived in the nearby bishop's palace, contributed to the cost of the new church and his family donated many of the fittings. St Catherine's (later St Catharine's) church was not in a populous area and, having been replaced by a new church at Wotton Pitch in 1915, was pulled down in 1921.

53 Barton Street chapel was erected just outside the east gate in 1699 for the Rev. James Forbes, a nonconformist minister, and his congregation. After Forbes's death in 1712 the congregation divided and from 1751 the chapel employed Unitarian ministers. In 1844 the wall obscuring the chapel from the street was removed and a new pedimented front was built. The chapel, which was remodelled internally in 1893, closed in 1968 and was demolished.

54 Southgate Congregational chapel originated in a schism at the Barton Street chapel *c*.1714. In 1730 the seceders built a meeting house next to their minister's house in lower Southgate Street and in 1850 the manse was pulled down and the chapel rebuilt on a grander scale. The view, published when the chapel reopened in 1851, shows its proximity to the docks. The chapel, which in 1973 united with the Presbyterian church in Park Road to form the James Forbes United Reformed Church, closed in 1974 and was demolished in 1981.

55 A Baptist church formed in 1813 became one of the largest nonconformist meetings in later 19th-century Gloucester. Its chapel opened in 1821 in Brunswick Road (formerly Parker's Row) was rebuilt in 1847 and 1872 to provide more accommodation. The chapel opened in 1872 is seen here with, on its right, the Raikes Memorial Hall built by the Baptists in 1884 to mark the centenary, in 1880, of the Sunday School movement. Both chapel and hall were demolished in the 1970s.

56 George Whitefield (1714-70), one of the pre-eminent preachers of his day, was born in Gloucester where his father Thomas was landlord of the *Bell*. His early experience of evangelical preaching was in the city's Independent meeting under its minister Thomas Cole. Whitefield, who introduced Methodism to Gloucester, was ordained in the city and preached his first sermon in St Mary de Crypt church in 1736. In 1788, some years after his death, his followers opened a chapel in St Mary's Square.

57 The Park Street mission, established by 1867, was based on a former Quaker meeting house. The meeting house, two converted cottages, had been ransacked in 1682 when its members were imprisoned and had been used by the Quakers until 1834 when they moved to a new building in Greyfriars. The old meeting house was replaced by a larger building for the mission in 1903.

Streets and Shops

58 In this early 20th-century view of Northgate Street the *Dolphin Vaults* stands on the left at the entrance to Dolphin Lane. The inn was demolished to make way for an extension of the Bon Marché store, further up the street, in 1909 and the lane was officially closed in 1926.

59 This photograph shows the top end of Northgate Street before the front of the *New Inn* was restored in 1925. Dentons, the business on the corner of New Inn Lane, had been founded in the early 1850s by Thomas Denton, a draper, in partnership with a Mr. Aldred.

60 The Bon Marché, in Northgate Street, was started in 1889 by John Rowe Pope as a drapery business and became Gloucester's largest department store. Extensions were built to the north (left) in 1909 and 1914 and the original store and an annexe beyond Oxbode Lane to the south were replaced in 1931 by a large new building forming part of the Oxbode development. The store was renamed Debenhams in the early 1970s.

61 Most buildings on the west side of the top end of Northgate Street were rebuilt in the 20th century. That occupied *c*.1960 by Geldart and John Collier had been one of several notable additions to the main streets in the early 19th century. Built *c*.1801 for the Old Bank, a business established by 1783, it had housed a branch of the Bank of England between 1826 and 1849.

62 Hare Lane, a narrow road leading northwards from Gloucester, was part of the town's northern suburbs in the Anglo-Saxon period. In the 1230s it was called the tanners' street. Later it was the main road to Tewkesbury until 1822, when Worcester Street was built to take traffic heading northwards from the city. The east side of Hare Lane contained many old timber-framed houses until slum clearance began in the area in the late 1930s.

63 The corn exchange in Southgate Street was built in 1856 on the site of an 18th-century market hall. Its portico was crowned by a statue of Ceres, the Roman goddess of agriculture, and its hall was used for public meetings and social events as well as for grain dealing. Corn merchants preferred to deal in the cattle market and the exchange was remodelled in 1893 to accommodate the city's post office. The building in the distance, where Southgate Street narrows at the entrance to Commercial Road, was built for the Gloucester Savings Bank in 1849.

64 In this view of Southgate Street the medieval parish church of St Mary de Crypt, rebuilt in the late 14th century, retains its tower battlements and pinnacles. They were removed later, in 1908. Beyond the church is the Old Crypt Schoolroom, built in 1539 and occupied until 1862 by the grammar school founded by John Cooke (d.1528), a wealthy mercer and alderman, and his wife Joan (d.c.1545).

65 This photograph, looking towards the Cross and Northgate Street, was taken after the electrification of the trams in 1904. The tram is bound for Hucclecote. The front of the corn exchange, in Southgate Street, dates from a rebuilding in 1893 when it became the city post office. It was demolished in 1938. The building to the right, occupied by the mercantile offices of Stubbs Ltd., was built after 1893.

66 In the later 19th century Gloucester spread southwards along the Bristol road beyond the junction of the Stroud road. While the land between the road and the canal, to the west, was used for industrial and commercial development, land east of the road was also filled with shops and houses, mostly terraced artisan cottages. This view of *c*.1910, looking south, includes S.J. Moreland's match factory of 1868 and the *Robin Hood* inn.

67 This picture of Eastgate Street in the mid-1890s shows, on the left and in the middle distance in its original position, the Eastgate market portico of 1856. On the right the building beyond the American & Canadian Stores became a cinema and theatre in 1911. Known from 1915 as the Hippodrome, it was given a new front in 1935 and, after being damaged by fire in 1955, was renamed the Gaumont in 1959. It closed in 1961.

68 One of Victorian Gloucester's more successful retailers was Robert Blinkhorn, who in 1843 opened a drapery shop in Eastgate Street. The store was expanded and it attracted many of these shoppers at the turn of the century. Opposite, on the right, the newly rebuilt *Saracen's Head* forms part of a line of impressive late 19th-century street fronts.

69 The appearance of this part of Eastgate Street, on the north side, was transformed at the end of the 19th century. The old gabled house next to the Bluecoat Hospital, occupied by the furniture business of Richard Margrett & Son, and the buildings to its left were replaced in 1888 and 1898 by new buildings for the National Provincial Bank and Lloyds Bank respectively. The Bluecoat Hospital was demolished in 1890 and the new Guildhall was built in its place.

70 These buildings in Eastgate Street, near the entrance to Barton Street, were demolished *c*.1970 during the development of the King's Walk shopping centre. Eastgate House, occupying the block between King Street and Dog Lane, was built soon after Gloucester's east gate was taken down in 1778. John Bellows built his printing works behind the house in 1873. Beyond, in the block between Dog Lane and Clarence Street, are the offices and showroom (partly visible) built in 1891 for the Gloucester Gaslight Co.

71 The Gloucester Co-operative and Industrial Society, started by railway and dock employees in 1860 for the purpose of retail trade, had 18 shops and a bakery in 1910. It also provided loans for house purchase and founded scholarships at the Schools of Science and Art. Of its two main shops, both in Brunswick Road, that built in 1877 on the corner of Barton Street (known popularly as Co-op Corner) was replaced in 1931.

72 These undistinguished buildings stood east of Charlton House and the public baths of 1891 near Barton Gates and were typical of the ribbon development along Barton Street. In the early 20th century they included the premises of the ice-cream makers Fazzi Toscano & Co., a business connected with Gloucester from the early 1880s. The buildings were removed for the construction of the Barton Pool, opened in 1966.

73 The outer part of Barton Street was built up with houses and shops from the mid-19th century. This section, on the south side, had been a pleasure ground called the Blenheim Gardens when it opened in 1812. Later renamed the Vauxhall Gardens, it was covered with terraced houses from 1863 when Blenheim Road and Vauxhall Road were laid out. The *Vauxhall* inn, on the left, had been part of the gardens.

74 Until the mid-18th century the upper part of Westgate Street, seen here looking towards the Cross in the late 19th century, was divided into two narrow lanes by buildings standing in its centre. They included two medieval parish churches, Holy Trinity and, higher up, St Mary de Grace, the latter of which was demolished in the 1650s. Among the shops shown here on the north side is that of the seed merchants George Winfield & Son. Higher up is the gabled building erected for the National Provincial Bank in 1843 and, just visible, the narrow entrance to St John's Lane (formerly Grace Lane).

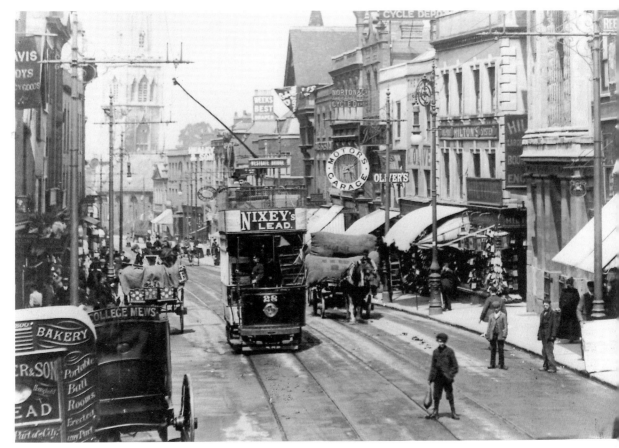

75 This photograph, looking down Westgate Street towards St Nicholas's church, was taken before 1917. On the north (right) side of the street the classical building above the entrance to College Court, in the foreground, was erected in the late 1830s for the County of Gloucester Bank.

76 This view of *c*.1900 looks down Westgate Street from the corner of Berkeley Street to the 12th-century parish church of St Nicholas (closed in 1967). The tower and spire of the church were built in the early 15th century and, as a result of subsidence, leant so heavily that in 1783 the spire's top was removed. The building below the entrance to Three Cocks Lane, and next but one above the church, was the former *King's Head* hotel. An important coaching inn and social centre, in the 18th century it had been patronised by the city corporation and in the mid-19th century it had been the election headquarters of the Liberal party.

77 A number of timber-framed houses in lower Westgate Street remained standing in the early 20th century. The two shown here, which were converted as a folk museum in 1935, included the house where Bishop John Hooper is believed to have lodged before his execution in 1555.

78 One building on the north side of lower Westgate Street not rebuilt or refronted in brick in the 18th or 19th centuries was that usually called the Duke of Norfolk's House. Built soon after 1724 and known for a time as Eagle Hall (the parapet once carried a large eagle), it was used as lodgings by Charles Howard, Duke of Norfolk (d.1815), an influential member of the corporation. The house had been subdivided and its ground floor converted as two shops by 1850.

Side Streets and Squares

79 Bull Lane, one of the main streets in medieval Gloucester, runs between upper Westgate Street and Longsmith Street. Known in the mid-13th century as Gore Lane, it had taken the name of the *Bull* inn by the early 18th century. Ernest Daniel Tandy was the inn's landlord in the late 1880s.

80 Oxbode or Oxbody Lane was one of several ancient streets on the east side of Northgate Street. In the 19th century, when it was also called Mitre Street, it became a slum. This view, looking east, also shows the Ebenezer Gospel Hall built in King Street in 1872. The houses were demolished in the late 1920s when the area was redeveloped to form the Oxbode and King's Square. The hall was demolished *c.*1970 when the King's Walk shopping centre incorporating King's Square was created.

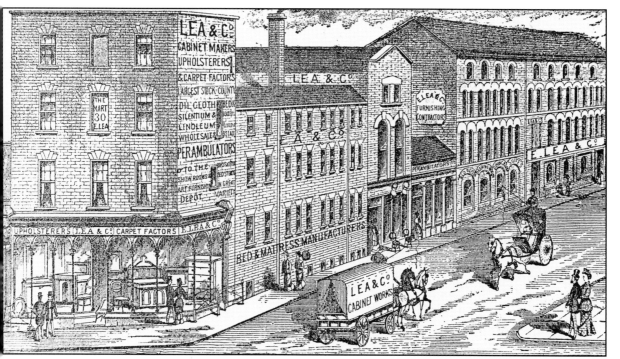

81 St Aldate Street, leading off Northgate Street, was named after the medieval parish church on its south side. The church was demolished in the mid-17th century. In the later 19th century the north side of the street was rebuilt piecemeal as workshops for Edwin Lea, who had started making furniture in a shop on the corner of Northgate Street in 1866.

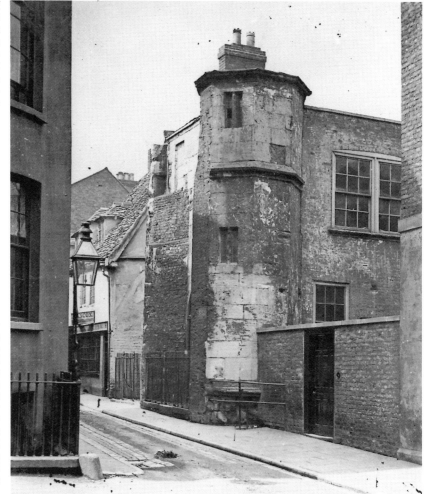

82 In the late Middle Ages two lanes led from the south side of the abbey (later cathedral) precinct into the town. The lower lane, entered through King Edward's gate, was known as King Edward's or St Edward's Lane and later as College Lane or Street. Part of the gateway dating from the early 16th century has survived but the buildings on the left side of the lane were demolished in 1892 so that the street could be widened to form a ceremonial approach to the cathedral from Westgate Street.

83 St Mary's Square, west of the cathedral precinct, formed around the churchyard of St Mary de Lode. The church, which took its name from a passage of the nearby Old Severn, dates from before the Norman Conquest and is Gloucester's oldest parish church. Its medieval chancel and tower survive but the aisled nave was pulled down in 1825 and replaced. Many houses around the square, including those on the north side shown here, were demolished in the 1950s and '60s. The monument is the memorial to Bishop John Hooper.

84 St Catherine Street, part of the northern suburbs of medieval Gloucester, was formerly called Wateringstead or Watering Street. It led to a place on the Old Severn where the townspeople drew water. The timber-framed houses on the corner of Park Street were demolished in the later 1950s. Thomas Enstone was landlord of the *Coach and Horses* in the 1890s.

85 Bearland was originally an open space in front of the castle used in the later Middle Ages as the site for the town's refuse. It was built up from 1644. This view from the corner of Longsmith Street and Berkeley Street shows the county magistrates' courts of 1908 on the corner of Barbican Road and other buildings demolished in the early 1960s to make way for a new police station.

86 George Street, originally called Church Street, was laid out by Charles Church in 1851 and ran from lower Northgate Street and London Road to the railway stations. In this photograph of *c*.1900, during the Boer War, ambulances made at the wagon works line the street. In the foreground, on the left and right, are two hotels, the *Wellington* and the *Gloucester*, built in the early 1850s and in the distance the tower and spire added to the Roman Catholic church of St Peter ad Vincula in 1868.

87 Tabby Pitt's Pool, created by digging for clay to make bricks for the viaduct carrying the South Wales railway across meadows north of the city, was filled in in 1889. This view from the north-west to the cathedral includes part of Priory Road, which was formed along the course of Dockham ditch (the Old Severn) in 1854. On the left are the parish church of St Catherine, consecrated in 1868, and, in front of it, the parish's National school for girls and infants, dating from 1876.

Public Buildings and Services

88 The Boothall stood south of Westgate Street behind an inn facing the street. The hall, used for courts and markets in the 13th and 14th centuries, was the first centre of town government and it became the shire hall for Gloucestershire. By the later 18th century the town's courts had moved to the Tolsey and in 1816, with the opening of the new Shire Hall, the Boothall ceased to have an administrative rôle. Shown here in 1847, it became stables for the inn and from the 1860s it was a place of popular entertainment. Despite many rebuildings some of the timber framing survived until 1957 when the hall was demolished.

89 The Shire Hall, in Westgate Street, opened next to the Boothall in 1816 as the new centre of county administration. Designed by Robert Smirke, its courtrooms were also used for the city's courts and its large assembly room became the city's main concert hall. This photograph was taken just before 1909 when the building was enlarged. It was rebuilt and much enlarged in the early 1960s.

90 The Tolsey, standing at the Cross on the corner of Southgate and Westgate Streets, was used for the business of town government perhaps as early as 1455. It was rebuilt several times, the last in 1751 when the Westgate Street front was adorned with a pediment displaying a carving of the city arms and civic maces. In 1893 the Tolsey, having been replaced by the new Guildhall in Eastgate Street, was demolished.

91 The county gaol was pulled down in 1787 to make way for a larger prison. The new prison, built on lines advocated by the penal reformer John Howard, was completed in 1791 and had buildings around three quadrangles, of which the south quadrangle is illustrated here. New buildings were added in 1826, when the prison area was extended eastwards to Barbican Road, and in the 1840s. The prison accommodated both sexes until *c.*1915 when it became an all-male establishment.

92 Gloucester's military associations go back several centuries. In the early 19th century the county yeomanry (later the Royal Gloucestershire Hussars) frequently trained there and a militia regiment was stationed in the city and between 1854 and 1856 barracks for the county militia were built north of the county prison near the river Severn. Although Gloucester did not become a garrison town under the military reforms of 1872, its military traditions continued and the barracks and the spa grounds were used frequently for drilling and reviewing troops. The barracks were demolished in the 1960s.

93 The workhouse of the Gloucester poor-law union was built in 1837 and 1838 by the board of guardians established in 1835 to administer the poor law in the city and surrounding villages. Designed by the partnership of George Gilbert Scott and W.B. Moffatt, the workhouse, in the later Great Western Road, was enlarged, a separate infirmary being completed next to it in 1852, and from 1912 buildings, including a new infirmary, were erected on the opposite side of the road. The city corporation took over the buildings in 1930 and the former workhouse is shown here, presumably with members of the corporation shortly before it was demolished in 1961.

94 In 1826 a memorial to John Hooper, Protestant bishop of Gloucester, was placed on the spot outside the cathedral precinct where he had been burned at the stake in front of St Mary's gate in 1555. Paid for by J.R. Cleland, an Ulsterman, it was replaced by this more imposing monument, paid for by public subscription and completed in 1863.

95 This house, which stood in a small square facing St Aldate's churchyard on the south side of St Aldate Street, had been Gloucester's post office in 1822. The office was housed from 1847 in the Tolsey and later in the Southgate Street corn exchange. A new central post office opened in King's Square in 1934.

96 In the 17th and 18th centuries firefighting equipment provided by the corporation was kept at churches and other places in the city. From 1838 the city's police force trained as a fire brigade but most firefighting in the later 19th century was by brigades employed by insurance companies. The brigade and engine of the Liverpool and London and Globe company are pictured in Southgate Street outside the company's office at the corner of Bell Lane.

97 In 1912 the corporation formed a brigade to operate firefighting equipment donated by two insurance companies and built a fire station in Bearland. The station, opened on 17 July 1913, was used until 1956, when a new fire station opened in Eastern Avenue, and was adapted as a transport museum in 1977. Bearland House, partly visible to the left, was one of the larger houses built in the city in the late 17th and early 18th centuries.

Inns and Hotels

98 The *Boothall* inn or hotel, in Westgate Street, stood in front of the Boothall on a site which was an inn before 1455. It was an important meeting place in the early 1740s, when a new pedimented street front was built, and for a time it was a coaching inn. The archway on the left led to the Boothall, which at the time of this photograph, *c.*1905, was a variety theatre and in 1907 became a cinema. The inn and hall were demolished in 1957.

99 The *New Inn*, in Northgate Street, was built not long before 1455 by Gloucester Abbey. A large timber-framed building with a galleried courtyard, it was Gloucester's leading inn in the early 17th century but it did not rank among the city's principal coaching inns of the 18th and 19th centuries. The timber street front, which had been covered over by 1850, was partly restored in 1925 when it accommodated two shops.

100 The *Ram*, in Northgate Street, was built by Gloucester Abbey in the early 16th century. Recorded from 1525, it stood opposite St John's church and, like the *New Inn*, had a courtyard reached from the street by a covered passage. The building, one of many timber-framed houses to survive in the city in the early 19th century, was demolished in 1865.

101 The *Bell*, in Southgate Street, was recorded from 1544. It became one of Gloucester's principal coaching inns and, by the later 1830s, was the meeting place for local Conservatives. Its long pedimented front, probably erected in 1793, was taken down in 1864 when the inn or hotel was rebuilt. The *Bell* closed in 1967 and was demolished during the construction of the Eastgate shopping centre.

Almshouses

102 The hospitals or almshouses of St Margaret and St Mary Magdalen on London Road were founded as lazar or leper houses outside the medieval town. St Margaret's, originally called St Sepulchre's, was governed by Gloucester Abbey in the mid-12th century and St Mary's, further out near Wotton Pitch, by Llanthony Priory. Both hospitals came under the control of the city corporation. In 1861 they were united and from 1862 their inmates were housed in a new building next to St Margaret's. The ancient almshouses, of which those of St Mary's, shown here, were arranged around a courtyard, were demolished.

103 St Margaret's and St Mary Magdalen's Hospitals had detached chapels, both dating from the 12th century. For several centuries they were used by local residents as well as by the almspeople. St Mary's chapel, shown here, stood south of the London road, which in 1821 was diverted to run between the chapel and the hospital buildings to the south. The chapel had been abandoned by the 1840s, when the almspeople attended St Margaret's chapel, and the nave was demolished in 1861. The chancel formed part of Hillfield Gardens in 1994.

104 According to tradition St Bartholomew's Hospital, in lower Westgate Street, was built in Henry II's reign on the approach to Gloucester from Westgate bridge as lodgings for the bridge's builders and for the sick. The largest of Gloucester's medieval hospitals, after 1564 it came under the patronage of the city corporation and housed 40 almspeople. St Bartholomew's, including its chapel, was rebuilt between 1787 and 1790 and remained an almshouse until 1971.

Hospitals

105 The Gloucester Infirmary was a county hospital founded in 1755 as a charitable institution. In 1761 it moved to a new building in lower Southgate Street and in 1788 it was visited by George III during his stay in Cheltenham. In 1878 it took over the work of an eye hospital in Market Parade and in 1909 Edward VII conferred the title of the Gloucestershire Royal Hospital and Eye Institution. In 1948 it united with the Gloucester City General Hospital in Great Western Road, where the new Gloucestershire Royal Hospital was built in the 1960s and '70s. The infirmary in Southgate Street, which as shown here included, on the right, a south wing added in 1825, was demolished in 1984.

106 Horton Road Hospital originated in a charitable scheme to provide an asylum for wealthy and poor patients. The county and city magistrates joined the scheme in 1813 and the asylum opened in new buildings at Wotton in 1823. The crescent contained rooms for wealthy patients and their servants and the wings rooms for poorer patients. From 1856 the asylum was run by the county and the city solely for the poor and it became known as the county asylum. A second county asylum opened at Coney Hill in 1884.

07 Barnwood House Hospital in Barnwood was a private mental hospital opened in 1860. Occupying new buildings attached to an early 19th-century villa on Ermin Street, the Roman road between Gloucester and Cirencester, it was originally for 60 patients. The accommodation, which reflected a degree of opulence, was later increased and in the mid-1890s the original house was rebuilt. A chapel was built in the grounds in 1869. The hospital closed in 1968 and its work continued on a much smaller scale at the nearby Manor House.

08 In 1867 a children's hospital opened in a new building on the Tewkesbury road between Kingsholm and Longford. The idea of Thomas Gambier Parry, it stood next to the first St Lucy's Home of Charity. Treatment was free and the nursing was undertaken initially by the sisters of St Lucy, an Anglican community founded by Gambier Parry, from 1872 by the sisters of St John the Baptist at Clewer in Berkshire, and from 1939 by the sisters of St John the Divine at Deptford in Kent. The hospital closed in 1947 and was demolished in 1979.

109 Smallpox claimed many lives i Victorian Gloucester. Mortality was greates in an outbreak which began in 1895 an spread among children in two schools an many households in the south of the city The corporation put up temporary building next to its isolation hospital near the Strou road and next to a cholera hospital near th docks. The epidemic, which abated in Jul 1896, was confined to Gloucester where claimed 434 lives, 280 of them childre under 10 years of age. The isolation hospital shown here during the epidemic, closed i 1903 on the opening of Over Hospital.

110 Walter Robert Hadwen (1854-1932) a doctor and anti-vivisectionist, settled i Gloucester following the 1896 smallpo epidemic to champion the anti-vaccinatio cause there and was elected to the cit council in 1898. In 1924, following the deat of one of his child patients from smallpox he was unsuccessfully prosecuted fo manslaughter. An active member of th Plymouth Brethren, he built Albion Hall i lower Southgate Street.

Education

111 Much of the credit for the Sunday School movement belongs to the Gloucester businessman and philanthropist Robert Raikes, who, in collaboration with the Rev. Thomas Stock, started Sunday schools in the city in 1780. Raikes (d.1811) used his newspaper, the *Gloucester Journal*, to promote the movement. The *Journal*, a weekly publication, had been founded by his father Robert (d.1757) and William Dicey in 1722. A statue of the younger Robert Raikes was erected in Gloucester Park in 1930, the 150th anniversary of the Sunday School movement.

112 A National school was opened in London Road in 1817 to provide boys and girls from all parts of the city with a church education. It was promoted by a diocesan committee headed by the bishop of Gloucester, Henry Ryder, and the foundation stone was laid in 1816 by the Duke of Welllington. Attendance fell from the 1830s, when the city parishes began opening their own National schools, and it became a boys' school. The number of pupils began to rise in the 1870s and the school was enlarged in 1879 and 1895. It closed in 1962.

113 (*above*) Among the National schools built in Gloucester in the 1830s and '40s was one in the Barton Street suburb in the area then known as Barton End. Opened in 1844, it served the parish of the new St James's church and much of the cost was borne by Thomas Hedley, the parish priest. Copies of this illustration, by the Cheltenham artist George Rowe, were sold to help pay for the building.

114 (*right*) In 1876 a school board was formed to ensure that Gloucester had enough elementary school places. The board, elected by ratepayers, had opened schools in Tredworth High Street and Widden Street by 1878 and it moved the Tredworth school to a new building on the corner of Tredworth Road in 1887. The new school, with room for 684 children, quickly became overcrowded and in 1911 it was enlarged.

115 The Derby Road schools for junior boys, junior girls, and infants were opened on 8 April 1907 by the mayor, Samuel Aitken. They were built by the city council, which had become the local education authority in 1903. From 1925 the buildings of the boys' and girls' schools housed the Central schools set up by the authority to provide technical and industrial training for children aged 11 and over.

116 The King's School, formerly known as the College school, was a boys' grammar school refounded under the control of the dean and chapter of Gloucester after the dissolution of St Peter's Abbey in 1540. The school, housed in the former abbey library, moved in 1849 to a new building on the north side of the cathedral and from 1891 it also occupied Paddock House in Pitt Street. At that time it had between fifty and sixty pupils. The completion of new buildings in Pitt Street in 1929 allowed an increase in the number of pupils, and later the school took over other buildings in and around the cathedral close.

117 By his will Sir Thomas Rich (d.1667), a baronet and a prosperous London merchant, founded a charity school for 20 boys in his native Gloucester. Sometimes called the Bluecoat Hospital, it opened in 1668 in a house in Eastgate Street under the management of the city corporation. In the 19th century the number of pupils grew considerably and in 1889 the school moved to Barton Street and in 1964, having become a secondary grammar school, to Elmbridge. The building in Eastgate Street, shown here, dated from a rebuilding in the years 1806-8 and was pulled down in 1890 to make way for the new Guildhall.

118 The pupils of Sir Thomas Rich were dressed in a blue uniform like that of Christ's Hospital, London (later at Horsham, West Sussex). Known as the Bluecoat schoolboys, they took part in civic ceremonies, including processions to the cathedral and the annual perambulation of the city boundaries. The last Bluecoat schoolboys, pictured here, attended the school until 1882 when it was reorganised as a school for 200 boys under a new foundation, the Gloucester United Endowed Schools.

119   The opening of the Girls' High school in Denmark Road took place on 14 January 1909. The school, founded by the United Schools governors in 1883, had been housed in Mynd House, Barton Street, until 1904 and in Bearland House until 1909. The city's second girl's high school was opened by the United Schools governors in Ribston Hall, Spa Road, in 1921.

120   The Schools of Science and Art were built in Brunswick Road by subscription in 1871 and 1872 with the support of county landholders, notably Thomas Gambier Parry of Highnam. The schools, which also housed a museum, were taken over by Gloucester corporation in 1896 and a public library was added on the left side between 1898 and 1900. From 1902 the museum was housed in the Price Memorial Hall erected on the right side in 1893.

121 The Gloucestershire College of Education, closed in 1980, originated as the Gloucestershire School of Cookery and Domestic Economy, opened in 1891. Renamed the Gloucestershire School of Domestic Science in 1900, it became one of the largest colleges outside London for training domestic science teachers. It moved from Quay Street to the nearby barracks in 1894 and, its curriculum having been expanded, to new buildings on the Cheltenham road in 1958.

122 St Lucy's Home of Charity trained girls and young women for domestic service. In that respect it was one of several institutions undertaking work of a missionary and reformatory character in the city. Among them was the Magdalen Asylum, originally founded in 1821, which from *c.*1900 occupied Picton House in Wellington Parade.

The Spa

123 Beginning in 1814 Sir James Jelf created a spa around springs in Rigney Stile Grounds on the south side of the city. Its pump room was opened to subscribers in 1815. The spa had begun to decline in popularity by the late 1820s and its grounds were acquired by the city corporation in 1861 and incorporated in a new public park. The medicinal springs were closed in 1894 and the pump room was demolished in 1960.

124 The building of fashionable houses near the spa began in 1816 following the laying out of Spa Road (originally called Norfolk Street) along the north side of the spa grounds. The first buildings included a hotel (later Ribston Hall) provided by the spa's owners. Sherborne House, one of the first houses in Spa Road, was built by the attorney John Chadborn and is seen here, in the centre. The side extensions had been added as separate dwellings by 1843.

125 The development of the Spa suburb in the early 1820s included the creation of Brunswick Square on a close called Gaudy Green west of Gloucester Place (later the south part of Brunswick Road), the road leading from the spa to the city. Beginning in 1822 terraced houses were built on three sides of the square. The west side is shown here.

126 Christ Church, Brunswick Square, was consecrated in 1823. A proprietary church for the wealthy residents of the Spa, it was built of stuccoed brick to a plain neo-classical design by the partnership of Thomas Rickman and Henry Hutchinson. This is a rare view of the church before 1890 when its appearance was transformed by the addition of a new vermillion terracotta west front.

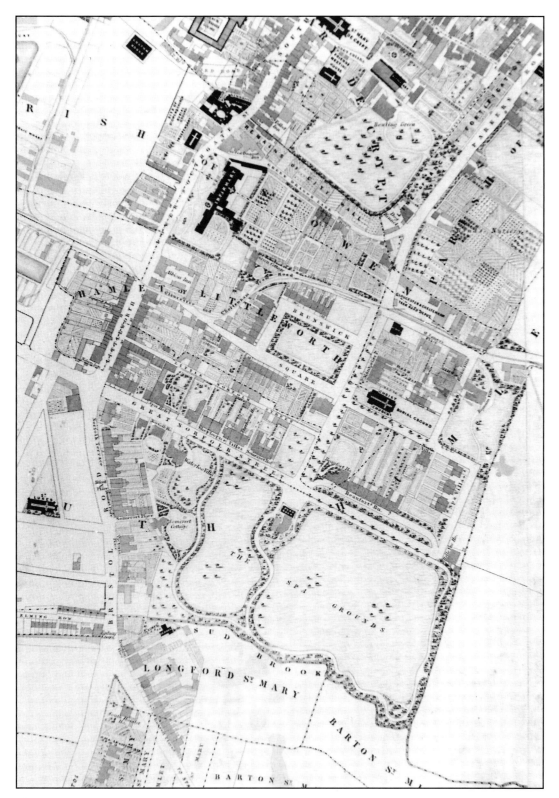

127 Arthur Causton's map of Gloucester in 1843 shows the Spa suburb's proximity to burgeoning commercial and industrial development to the west (left). The new custom house in the docks (top left) opened in 1845 and Commercial Road, the proposed route from Southgate Street, was completed in 1847. The nearby city gaol was built in the 1780s and closed in 1858. Buildings at High Orchard (bottom left) included terraced houses in Elming Row (originally called Anti-Dry-Rot Street). St Luke's church and, to the south-east, school were provided in 1841 and 1843 respectively by the Rev. Samuel Lysons of Hempsted Court.

Housing

128 Marybone House, Bearland, was built in the mid-17th century and was enlarged by the lawyer Benjamin Hyett, the owner in 1686. The Hyetts retained the house after they became landowners in Painswick. The main front, not shown, looked towards the castle grounds where a garden created in the 1740s with a pagoda was covered in the 1780s with part of the new county gaol. The house became Gloucester's main police station in 1858.

129 Among the larger houses built in Gloucester after 1660 was that later called Elton House. Built soon after 1681, it was on the south side of Barton Street and had an elaborate garden in the mid-18th century when the physician Charles Greville lived there. In the early 20th century it was the residence of Ernest Dykes Bower, a surgeon and oculist.

30 In the 19th century cottages were built in the back yards of many older houses to accommodate part of Gloucester's growing population. The photograph of Glendinning's and Cox's Passages in Hare Lane *c*.1935 shows a typical row of 19th-century slum cottages. The older timber range occupied as dwellings was the rear wing of the early 16th-century *Old Raven* tavern, the main part of which was later restored for use as an old people's centre.

31 Many of the small enclosed courts built in Gloucester in the 19th century were in the lower Westgate Street area, which had become the most congested and insanitary part of the city by 1850. This court was behind the *Elephant and Castle* inn in Quay Street.

132 Gloucester's 19th-century suburbs included large areas of closely packed streets filled with small terraced houses and factories. This row of houses in High Orchard Street and several other dwellings were burnt out by a fire at a nearby furniture factory in 1912.

133 The streets of small terraced houses built in the mid-19th century were interspersed with pockets of more commodious dwellings, some built for philanthropic motives. Several in the High Street area of Tredworth were built by a land society formed by Gloucester Liberals in 1852. The society developed two small estates there, these cottages in Melbourne Street and dated 1855 forming part of its Painswick Road estate.

134 Alvin Street, known in the early 13th century as Fete Lane, was outside the medieval town and ran from the London road to Alvin gate at the entrance to the Hare Lane suburb. Houses in the area were destroyed at the start of the 1643 siege and, in the first large-scale development of working-class housing of the 19th century, the land on the north-east (right) side was filled with terraced streets from 1823. Most of the streets were cleared in the 1960s when new housing was provided in the area.

Transport

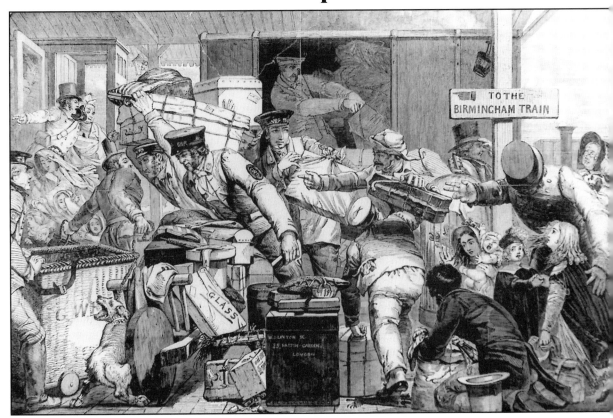

135 (*above*) When railway traffic began between Bristol and Birmingham in 1844, passengers and goods had to change trains at Gloucester, where there was a break of gauge. The inconvenience, caricatured in the *Illustrated London News*, lasted until 1854 when the Midland Railway converted the Bristol line to the narrow gauge and built the Tuffley or Barton loop line into its Gloucester terminus. In 1896 the company built a station (later called Eastgate), some way to the south-east, which through trains could use without reversing. With the closure of that station in 1975 Gloucester's railways reverted to the pattern of the 1840s.

136 (*right*) In 1851 over 150 Gloucester men worked on the railways. That number increased in the following decades as the railway network expanded and more local branch lines opened. The Great Western Railway rebuilt its station between 1887 and 1889 and W.F. Marvin was stationmaster at the time of this photograph in 1910. The station (later called Central) had the Midland Railway's terminus as a neighbour until 1896 when that company's new station opened some way to the south-east. A long footbridge connecting the two stations remained in use until 1975.

137 (*above*) The complex railway network created in Gloucester in the mid-19th century included level crossings in many streets. One was Barton Gates in Barton Street and this view of *c*.1910, looking from Park Road into Station Road, shows the entrance to the pedestrian subway and the signal box at the crossing. Beyond is the foundry of Kell & Co., makers of agricultural implements, and, to the left, Eastgate station. Also visible is the west end of All Saints' church, completed in 1875 to designs by Sir George Gilbert Scott.

138 In the late 19th century Gloucester's transport services included buses operated by George Symonds from College Mews in Hare Lane. His vehicles, pictured here in Worcester Street, also served the outlying villages of Hucclecote and Tuffley. This photograph also shows the upper part of a chapel built by members of the Methodist New Connexion in 1857. It closed in the mid-1890s.

139 Horse-drawn trams became part of the city's transport system in 1879. They were run by the Gloucester Tramways Co. and the service along Barton Street ran to a terminus in India Road, where this photograph was taken. The tram system was enlarged several times but its owners, from 1881 the City of Gloucester Tramways Co., had financial difficulties and were bought out by the city corporation in 1902.

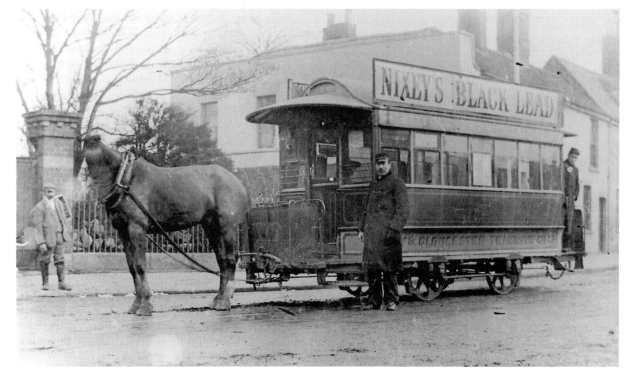

140 Following its purchase by the corporation, the tram system was improved and converted to electric traction. Those works attracted great crowds at the Cross. The new service, inaugurated in 1904, also ran beyond the city boundary along Ermin Street to Hucclecote. The electric trams proved a serious drain on the corporation's finances and in 1929 and 1933 the services were withdrawn and replaced by motor buses.

141 The electric tram service between the Cross and Westgate bridge was discontinued in 1917. This photograph, taken near the bottom of Westgate Street below the junction of Lower Quay Street, looks westwards and shows the *Admiral Benbow*, one of several buildings demolished in 1909 to widen that section of the road.

Politics and Politicians

Who wants a Ticket for Soup?

DICKY, after losing HOPE, catches a TURTLE!!

Gentlemen, Allow me to introduce to your notice Alderman Sir Robert Turtle, who has promised to SHELL OUT and who has come all the way from the City of London. Look at him! He's REAL TURTLE Gentlemen, and full of Fat GREEN FAT, Gentlemen!!!

142 By the mid-19th century parliamentar and municipal elections in Gloucester wer often accompanied by widespread bribery an other improprieties. Such malpractices led t recrimination and provided ammunition fo cartoonists. For the 1857 parliamentary contes the Conservatives chose Sir Robert Carden, wealthy London stockbroker, to regain the se Henry Thomas Hope had lost in 1852. Carde here portrayed as a turtle, topped the poll afte buying many votes.

143 Following the 1859 parliamentar election, one of the most corrupt ever held the city, the successful Liberal candidate W.P. Price and C.J. Monk, were unseated fo bribery. Gloucester remained unrepresented Parliament until 1862 and its reputation fo corrupt politics, strengthened in 1880 whe the Liberal Thomas Robinson was disqualifie from taking his seat, lingered until the Firs World War. Gloucester's representation wa reduced from two seats to one in 1885.

Election Sketches – No 7.

GLOUCESTER CITY RACES. 1859.

The Race for the Parliament Plate.

Mr W.P. Price's Gloucester Glory.   Mr C.J. Monk's Young Liberal.   SIR R.W.Carden's True Blue.

True Blue (who was overweighted and, as usual, shewed temper) kicked off his rider early in the Race and left his opponents to win in a Canter. Betting 100 to 1 agst. True Blue.

Published by W. Henley, Southgate-st. Gloster - Price 6d

144 William Philip Price (1817-91) of Tibberton Court was Gloucester's leading timber merchant and a member of its Unitarian church. A Liberal, he represented the city in Parliament in the years 1852-9 and 1865-73. He was also chairman of the Midland Railway and resigned as M.P. in 1873 on his appointment as a Railway Commissioner.

145 Thomas Robinson (1827-97), a corn and manure merchant who ran a business started by his cousin John Robinson, was first elected to the city council in 1858 and became the leader of Gloucester's Liberals. The dominant personality in the city's politics in the later 19th century, he was mayor four times and M.P. for Gloucester between 1889 and 1895. He was knighted in 1894.

146 John Ward (1820-95), a native of Gloucester, retired from business as a builder in the mid-1860s to devote himself to public service. A member of the city council from 1865 until his death and its only Conservative member between 1869 and 1871, he was popular among working men. Elected mayor in 1887 and 1894, he died, during his second term, at Bohanam House, Wotton. In his later years he had provided a Christmas treat for the poor and he left £6,000 as an endowment for charitable purposes.

147 James Bruton (1848-1933) started in business with his father Henry, an auctioneer, and in 1869 joined his brother-in-law James Reynolds at Albert Mills. A Conservative member of the city council from 1907 and mayor nine times, he was knighted in 1916 and was M.P. for Gloucester 1918-24.

148 New offices called Victoria Chambers were opened in Bell Lane in 1901 for the Gloucester Conservative Benefit Society. Founded in 1880 as a provident society for working men, it had over 7,000 members in 1901. The Liberals had a similar but smaller society, founded in 1887. The Conservative society moved to a new building in Barton Street in 1936 and merged with its parent society in Stroud in 1968 to form the Original Holloway Society.

149 Suffolk House, a large early 19th-century residence in Greyfriars, became the Liberal club in 1890. The house, which had been used from the mid-1820s by a number of schools, accommodated a lodge of the Good Templars from 1927 and the children's library from 1938. It was demolished in the later 1960s to make way for a market hall forming part of the new Eastgate shopping centre. A bowling green laid in front of the house for the Liberal club in 1921 remained in use in 1994.

Music and Literature

150 Samuel Sebastian Wesley (1819-76), a distinguished musician and composer of church music, was appointed cathedral organist in 1865 after the dean and chapter had invited him to examine candidates to succeed John Amott in the post. Wesley died at his residence in the cathedral close.

151 The poet, critic and dramatist William Ernest Henley (1849-1903) was the son of a Gloucester bookseller and was educated at the Crypt grammar school. A sufferer from tubercular disease, he had part of his left leg amputated at the age of 16 and went to Edinburgh in 1873 for surgery. He settled in London and inspired the character Long John Silver in Robert Louis Stevenson's *Treasure Island*.

152 The main musical and social event in the city was the triennial Three Choirs Festival, originally the meeting of the choirs of Gloucester, Hereford and Worcester cathedrals. In the later 19th century the festival included choral services and oratorio performances in the cathedral and secular evening concerts in the Shire Hall assembly room. Cathedral performances were usually directed by the cathedral organist and at this rehearsal for the 1901 festival the organist Alfred Herbert Brewer occupies the rostrum and Charles Harford Lloyd, organist 1876-82, is seated to the left. Brewer, a native of Gloucester, held the post from 1896. He was knighted in 1926 and died two years later.

Recreation and Leisure

153 Gloucester Park, opened in 1862 on the south side of the city, was laid out by the corporation for recreation. It incorporated the spa grounds, to the west, which were used by many new sports clubs in the later 19th century. The Eastgate market fountain was moved to the park at the expense of C.J. Monk, a former M.P., and Charles Walker, a timber merchant and industrialist, built a bandstand there in 1863. The church overlooking the park is that built in the early 1870s by Presbyterians as a memorial to the 18th-century evangelist George Whitefield.

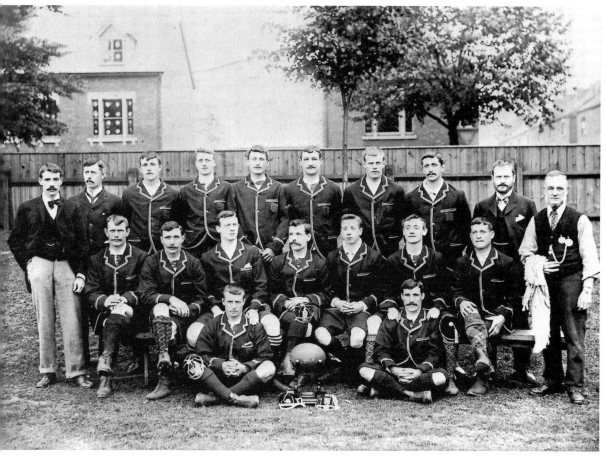

54 Gloucester Football Club was formed in 1873 to play rugby union football. It played regularly at the spa grounds ntil 1891 when its ground at Kingsholm was opened. These players were its principal team in the mid-1890s. With later uccesses many club members obtained international honours and the Kingsholm ground became a mecca for rugby nthusiasts.

155 (*above*) Association football or soccer rules were introduced to Gloucester in 1886 and Gloucester City Association Football Club traces its origins to a club formed in 1889. The team during the 1897-8 season is shown here. The club had a chequered early history and in 1925 it was revived after a lapse of several years. It had a succession of homes, including from 1935 a ground at Longlevens and from 1964 a stadium in Horton Road, before moving to Sudmeadow Road.

156 (*right*) From the day of its consecration in 1841 St James's church, Upton Street, was a centre of missionary work in the outer Barton Street suburb. Under Frederick Billett, vicar from 1895, a committee (here pictured with him in 1899) was formed to run a bible class and a social club for working men. From 1901 the club met in a new building on a site, at the corner of lower Barton Street and Hatfield Road, donated by John Dearman Birchall of Bowden Hall, Upton St Leonards.

157 (*above*) Gloucester's public baths, opened in Barton Street in 1891, included two indoor swimming pools, once convertible for use as a gymnasium, and a suite of Turkish baths. The main pool, shown here during the opening ceremony performed on 30 July by the mayor Joseph John Seekings, was retained as a training pool after 1966 when the new Barton pool opened on an adjoining site.

158 (*above*) Gloucester had several roller-skating rinks before the First World War, including one opened in the Boothall in 1876. The rink illustrated here was opened on 4 September 1909 by the mayor James Bruton in a former tram depot in India Road. Known as the Empress rink, it closed *c*.1917 and was reopened for a period in 1930.

159 (*right*) For many years pleasure boats plied the river Severn between Gloucester and Tewkesbury and Worcester. The steam launch *Berkeley Castle*, which is moored at a new landing stage above Westgate bridge possibly for a works outing, was probably built at Gloucester by Charles Priday in 1879. The *Windsor Castle*, her sister, was launched by Priday in 1887. The bridge, that completed in 1816, was demolished in 1941. The horses on Oxlease probably worked on the river towpath.

160 (*above*) The Theatre Royal, so called from the late 1830s, was the most successful theatre built in Gloucester in the later 18th century. Erected in 1791 by the impresario John Boles Watson and enlarged in 1859 by John Blinkhorn, it was used as a variety theatre and picture house in the early 20th century. It had closed by 1922 when part of the building was demolished and the rest converted as a store.

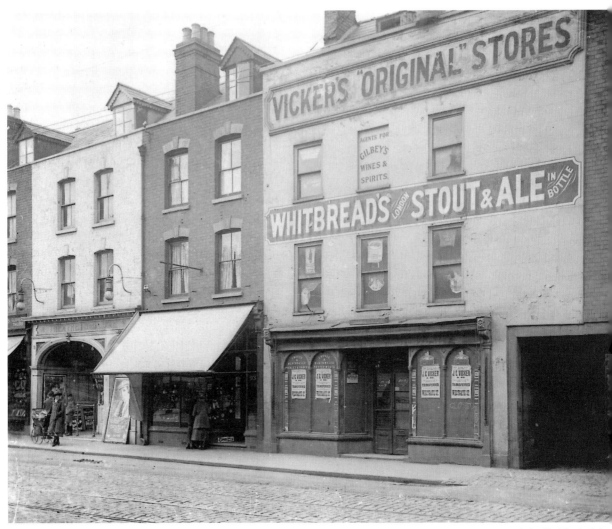

161 The Theatre de Luxe cinema, the building on the left of this group in lower Northgate Street, was originally Frederick Goddard's piano factory. The factory was used as an assembly room by 1881 and was converted as a cinema in 1909. It closed after a fire in 1939. A classical portico added in 1922 survived as the street front until 1959.

Events and Incidents

162 In 1867 a drinking fountain was erected in the wall of the cattle market opposite Clarence Street. It was paid for by Catherine Howell, a local spinster, and she attended its inauguration.

163 One of the major events of 1867 was the launch of the *Gloucester*, a lifeboat bought for the National Lifeboat Institution with money raised locally and destined for service at Falmouth. The launch, on 9 April, was preceded by a procession through the streets and took place in the Victoria dock. It was witnessed by a large crowd, including many people on the roof of the custom house and a few perched on the roof of City Mills.

164 Gloucester's celebrations for Edward VII's coronation in 1902 included the planting of an oak tree in the park. The ceremony, on 4 August, was performed by the mayor, Samuel Bland, and his wife in the presence of the bishop, Charles Ellicott, the city's M.P., Russell Rea, and the mayors of Cheltenham and Tewkesbury. Bland was proprietor and founder in 1876 of the *Citizen*, Gloucester's most successful daily newspaper.

165 The Royal Agricultural Show held in Gloucester in 1909 provided the occasion, on 23 June, for the first formal visit to the city by a reigning monarch since 1788. After arriving by train at the G.W.R. station, Edward VII was taken to the Guildhall, in front of which representatives of the city and the county presented loyal addresses. Following that reception the king toured part of the city before proceeding to the Oxlease showground on Alney Island.

166 Throughout the 20th century Gloucester took great pride from being the home of the Gloucestershire Regiment, usually known as the Glosters. In 1911, 25 specially chosen members of the regiment's 5th battalion were on service for George V's coronation. Here they are seen on parade in the Gloucester barracks before setting out for London. In 1953 the honorary freedom of Gloucester was conferred on Lieutenant-Colonel James Carne, who in 1951 had commanded the Glosters' 1st battalion at the battle of Imjin River, Korea.

167 In this picture of *c*.1902 the diver is probably about to inspect the gates of the lock between the docks' main basin and the river Severn. The original double lock had been replaced by a deeper single chamber in 1892. Behind the spectators is the canal company's North Warehouse, completed in 1827.

168 On 7 September 1912 part of the river bank behind the prison subsided, damaging the wall at the entrance to the lock leading to the docks. As a result some boats had to moor upstream at the city quay where a crane installed by the corporation as part of improvements to the quay in the later 1880s was in use. The photograph shows part of Castle Meads on the opposite side of the river.

169 Gloucester Chamber of Commerce, founded in 1839, became the principal businessman's association in the city. On 24 July 1912 its members and their wives visited Tibberton Court at the invitation of Morgan Philips Price, a director of the timber merchants Price, Walker & Co. Seated centre is Rosa Bruton, wife of the association's vice-president James Bruton, who is standing behind her and to the right. Price, seated left of Mrs. Bruton, was prospective Liberal parliamentary candidate for Gloucester but he later joined the Labour Party and at the general election of 1922 failed narrowly to take the Gloucester seat from Bruton. He was M.P. for the Forest of Dean 1935-59.

170 An annual masonic festival held in Gloucester on 28 May 1912 became the occasion for laying the foundation stone of a new church, St Catharine's, at Wotton Pitch. The ceremony, watched by several hundred freemasons and many clergy including the bishop, was performed by Michael Edward Hicks Beach, Viscount St Aldwyn, the provincial grand master of Gloucestershire.

171 On 2 October 1915 a procession was held in Gloucester to recruit workers for the wagon works, then being used as a munitions factory. The procession passed the prison and the Gloucestershire School of Domestic Science, then at the barracks. That part of the prison visible here, the western range of the 1791 building, was demolished a few years later.